Learn French with The Memories of a Poor Devil

HypLern Interlinear Project
www.hyplern.com

First edition: 2025, June

Author: Octave Mirbeau
Translation: Kees van den End
Foreword: Camilo Andrés Bonilla Carvajal PhD

ISBN: 978-1-989643-08-2

kees@hyplern.com
www.hyplern.com

Learn French with The Memories of a Poor Devil

Interlinear French to English

Author
Octave Mirbeau

Translation
Kees van den End

HypLern Interlinear Project
www.hyplern.com

The HypLern Method

Learning a foreign language should not mean leafing through page after page in a bilingual dictionary until one's fingertips begin to hurt. Quite the contrary, through everyday language use, friendly reading, and direct exposure to the language we can get well on our way towards mastery of the vocabulary and grammar needed to read native texts. In this manner, learners can be successful in the foreign language without too much study of grammar paradigms or rules. Indeed, Seneca expresses in his sixth epistle that "Longum iter est per praecepta, breve et efficax per exempla[1]."

The HypLern series constitutes an effort to provide a highly effective tool for experiential foreign language learning. Those who are genuinely interested in utilizing original literary works to learn a foreign language do not have to use conventional graded texts or adapted versions for novice readers. The former only distort the actual essence of literary works, while the latter are highly reduced in vocabulary and relevant content. This collection aims to bring the lively experience of reading stories as directly told by their very authors to foreign language learners.

Most excited adult language learners will at some point seek their teachers' guidance on the process of learning to read in the foreign language rather than seeking out external opinions. However, both teachers and learners lack a general reading technique or strategy. Oftentimes, students undertake the reading task equipped with nothing more than a bilingual dictionary, a grammar book, and lots of courage. These efforts often end in frustration as the student builds mis-constructed nonsensical sentences after many hours spent on an aimless translation drill.

Consequently, we have decided to develop this series of interlinear translations intended to afford a comprehensive edition of unabridged texts. These texts are presented as they were originally written with no changes in word choice or order. As a result, we have a translated piece conveying the true meaning under every word from the original work. Our readers receive then two books in just one volume: the original version and its translation.

The reading task is no longer a laborious exercise of patiently decoding unclear and seemingly complex paragraphs. What's more, reading becomes an enjoyable and meaningful process of cultural, philosophical and linguistic learning. Independent learners can then acquire expressions and vocabulary while understanding pragmatic and socio-cultural dimensions of the target language by reading in it rather than reading about it.

Our proposal, however, does not claim to be a novelty. Interlinear translation is as old as the Spanish tongue, e.g. "glosses of [Saint] Emilianus", interlinear bibles in Old German, and of course James Hamilton's work in the 1800s. About the latter, we remind the readers, that as a revolutionary freethinker he promoted the publication of Greco-Roman classic works and further pieces in diverse languages. His effort, such as ours, sought to lighten the exhausting task of looking words up in large glossaries as an educational practice: "if there is any thing which fills reflecting men with melancholy and regret, it is the waste of mortal time, parental money, and puerile happiness, in the present method of pursuing Latin and Greek[2]".

Additionally, another influential figure in the same line of thought as Hamilton was John Locke. Locke was also the philosopher and translator of the Fabulae AEsopi in an interlinear plan. In 1600, he was already suggesting that interlinear texts, everyday communication, and use of the target language could be the most appropriate ways to achieve language learning:

> ...the true and genuine Way, and that which I would propose, not only as the easiest and best, wherein a Child might, without pains or Chiding, get a Language which others are wont to be whipt for at School six or seven Years together...[3]

---

1   "The journey is long through precepts, but brief and effective through examples". Seneca, Lucius Annaeus. (1961) Ad Lucilium Epistulae Morales, vol. I. London: W. Heinemann.

2   In: Hamilton, James (1829?) History, principles, practice and results of the Hamiltonian system, with answers to the Edinburgh and Westminster reviews; A lecture delivered at Liverpool; and instructions for the use of the books published on the system. Londres: W. Aylott and Co., 8, Pater Noster Row. p. 29.

3   In: Locke, John. (1693) Some thoughts concerning education. Londres: A. and J. Churchill. pp. 196-7.

Who can benefit from this edition?

We identify three kinds of readers, namely, those who take this work as a search tool, those who want to learn a language by reading authentic materials, and those attempting to read writers in their original language. The HypLern collection constitutes a very effective instrument for all of them.

1. For the first target audience, this edition represents a search tool to connect their mother tongue with that of the writer's. Therefore, they have the opportunity to read over an original literary work in an enriching and certain manner.

2. For the second group, reading every word or idiomatic expression in its actual context of use will yield a strong association between the form, the collocation, and the context. This will have a direct impact on long term learning of passive vocabulary, gradually building genuine reading ability in the original language. This book is an ideal companion not only to independent learners but also to those who take lessons with a teacher. At the same time, the continuous feeling of achievement produced during the process of reading original authors both stimulates and empowers the learner to study[1].

3. Finally, the third kind of reader will notice the same benefits as the previous ones. The proximity of a word and its translation in our interlinear texts is a step further from other collections, such as the Loeb Classical Library. Although their works might be considered the most famous in this genre, the presentation of texts on opposite pages hinders the immediate link between words and their semantic equivalence in our native tongue (or one we have a strong mastery of).

---

1   Some further ways of using the present work include:

1. As you progress through the stories, focus less on the lower line (the English translation). Instead, try to read through the upper line, staying in the foreign language as long as possible.

2. Even if you find glosses or explanatory footnotes about the mechanics of the language, you should make your own hypotheses on word formation and syntactical functions in a sentence. Feel confident about inferring your own language rules and test them progressively. You can also take notes concerning those idiomatic expressions or special language usage that calls your attention for later study.

3. As soon as you finish each text, check the reading in the original version (with no interlinear or parallel translation). This will fulfil the main goal of this

collection: bridging the gap between readers and original literary works, training them to read directly and independently.

Why interlinear?

Conventionally speaking, tiresome reading in tricky and exhausting circumstances has been the common definition of learning by texts. This collection offers a friendly reading format where the language is not a stumbling block anymore. Contrastively, our collection presents a language as a vehicle through which readers can attain and understand their authors' written ideas.

While learning to read, most people are urged to use the dictionary and distinguish words from multiple entries. We help readers skip this step by providing the proper translation based on the surrounding context. In so doing, readers have the chance to invest energy and time in understanding the text and learning vocabulary; they read quickly and easily like a skilled horseman cantering through a book.

Thereby we stress the fact that our proposal is not new at all. Others have tried the same before, coming up with evident and substantial outcomes. Certainly, we are not pioneers in designing interlinear texts. Nonetheless, we are nowadays the only, and doubtless, the best, in providing you with interlinear foreign language texts.

Handling instructions

Using this book is very easy. Each text should be read at least three times in order to explore the whole potential of the method. The first phase is devoted to comparing words in the foreign language to those in the mother tongue. This is to say, the upper line is contrasted to the lower line as the following example shows:

Quelquefois,	il	était	plus	bref.
Sometimes	he	was	more	brief

The second phase of reading focuses on capturing the meaning and sense of the original text. As readers gain practice with the method, they should be able to focus on the target language without getting distracted by the translation. New users of the method, however, may find it helpful to cover the translated lines with a piece of paper as illustrated in the image below. Subsequently, they try to understand the meaning of every word, phrase, and entire sentences in the target language itself, drawing on the translation only when necessary. In this phase, the reader should resist the temptation to look at the translation for every word. In doing so, they will find that they are able to understand a good portion of the text by reading directly in the target language, without the crutch of the translation. This is the skill we are looking to train: the ability to read and understand native materials and enjoy them as native speakers do, that being, directly in the original language.

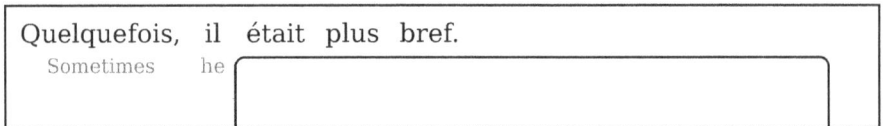

Quelquefois, il était plus bref.
Sometimes   he

In the final phase, readers will be able to understand the meaning of the text when reading it without additional help. There may be some less common words and phrases which have not cemented themselves yet in the reader's brain, but the majority of the story should not pose any problems. If desired, the reader can use an SRS or some other memorization method to learning these straggling words.

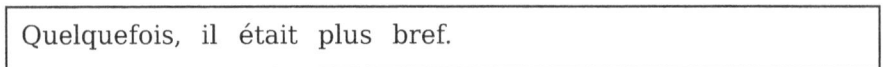

Quelquefois, il était plus bref.

Above all, readers will not have to look every word up in a dictionary to read a text in the foreign language. This otherwise wasted time will be spent concentrating on their principal interest. These new readers will tackle authentic texts while learning their vocabulary and expressions to use in further communicative (written or oral) situations. This book is just one work from an overall series with the same purpose. It really helps those who are afraid of having "poor vocabulary" to feel confident about reading directly in the language. To all of them and to all of you, welcome to the amazing experience of living a foreign language!

Additional tools

Check out shop.hyplern.com or contact us at info@hyplern.com for free mp3s (if available) and free empty (untranslated) versions of the eBooks that we have on offer.

For some of the older eBooks and paperbacks we have Windows, iOS and Android apps available that, next to the interlinear format, allow for a pop-up format, where hovering over a word or clicking on it gives you its meaning. The apps also have any mp3s, if available, and integrated vocabulary practice.

Visit the site hyplern.com for the same functionality online. This is where we will be working non-stop to make all our material available in multiple formats, including audio where available, and vocabulary practice.

Table of Contents

I

Ces pages que j'écris ne sont point une
These pages that I write not are at all an

autobiographie selon les normes littéraires.
autobiography according to the standards literary

Ayant vécu de peu, sans bruit, sans nul
Having lived of bit without noise without any
little

événement romanesque, toujours solitaire, même
event romantic always lonely even

dans ma famille, même au milieu de mes amis,
in my family even at the middle of my friends

même au milieu des foules un instant
even at the middle of the crowds a moment

coudoyées, je n'ai pas la vanité de penser
elbowed I not have -not- the vanity of to think
squished in between

que ma vie puisse offrir le moindre intérêt, ou le
that my life can offer the least interest or the

plus petit agrément, à être racontée.
most little approval to be narrated

Je n'attends donc, de ce travail, nulle gloire, nul
I do not expect then of this work any glory any

argent, ni la consolation de songer que je
silver neither the consolation of to think that I

puisse émouvoir l'âme de quelqu'un.
can move the soul of someone

Et pourquoi quelqu'un sur la terre se
And why someone on the earth himself

préoccuperait-il du silencieux insecte que je suis
would occupy of the silent insect that I am

? Je suis, dans le monde qui m'entoure de son
? I am in the world which surrounds me with its

immensité, un trop négligeable atome.
immensity a too negligible atom

Volontairement, ou par surprise, je ne sais,
Willingly or by surprise I (do) not know

j'ai rompu tous les liens qui m'attachaient à la
I have broken all the bonds which attached me to the

solidarité humaine ; j'ai refusé la part d'action,
solidarity human ; I have refused the side of action

utile ou malfaisante, qui échoit à tout être
useful or evil which falls to all being

vivant. Je n'existe ni en moi, ni dans les
alive I not exist neither in me nor in the

autres, ni dans le rythme le plus infime de
others nor in the rhythm the most minuscule of

l'universelle harmonie. Je suis cette chose
the universal harmony I am this thing

inconcevable et peut-être unique : rien ! j'ai
inconceivable and maybe unique : nothing ! I have

des bras, l'apparence d'un cerveau, les insignes
of the arms the appearance of a brain the signs

d'un sexe ; et rien n'est sorti de
of a gender ; and nothing not is come out of

cela, rien, pas même la mort ! Et si la
that nothing not even -the- death ! And if -the-

nature m'est si persécutrice, c'est que je tarde,
nature me is so tormentress this is that I delay
it is because

trop longtemps sans doute, à lui restituer ce
too long without doubt to her return this

petit tas de fumier, cette mince pincée de
little heap of manure this thin pinch of

pourriture qu'est mon corps, et de tant de
decay that is my body and of so many of

formes, charmantes, qui sait ?... tant
forms charming who knows ?... so many

d'organismes curieux attendent de naître, pour
of organisms curious wait of to be born for

perpétuer la vie dont, en réalité, je ne fais
to perpetuate the life of which in reality I not make

rien, sinon que l'interrompre. Qu'importe donc si
nothing if not than it interrupt Who cares then if

j'ai   pleuré, si,   du   soc   de mes   ongles,
I have   cried   if   of the   ploughshare   of   my   fingernails
edge

j'ai   parfois   labouré   ma   sanglante   poitrine !...
I have   sometimes   worked   my   bloody   chest   !...
scratched

Au   milieu   de   l'universelle   souffrance,   que   sont
At the   middle   of   the universal   pain   what   are

mes   pleurs ?   Que   signifie   ma   voix   déchirée   de
my   tears   ?   What   means   my   voice   torn   of

sanglots   ou   de   rires,   parmi   ce   grand   lamento   qui
sobs   or   of   laughs   among   this   large   lamento   which

secoue   les   mondes   affolés   par   l'impénétrable
shakes   the   worlds   distraught   by   the impenetrable

énigme   de   la   matière   ou   de   la   divinité ?
enigma   of   the   material   or   of   the   divinity   ?

Si   j'ai   dramatisé   ces   quelques   souvenirs   de
If   I have   dramatized   these   some   memories   of
few

l'enfance   qui   fut   mienne,   ce   n'est   pas   pour
the childhood   which   was   (the) mine   this   not is   -not-   for

qu'on   me plaigne,   qu'on   m'admire ou qu'on
that one me   pities   (for) that one admires me   or   that one

me haïsse. Je sais que je   n'ai   droit à aucun de
me   hates   I know that I not have right at   any   of

ces sentiments dans le cœur des hommes. Et
these   feelings   in   the heart of the   men   And

 qu'en   ferais-je ?
what of it would I make ?

Est-ce la voix du suprême orgueil qui parle en
Is this   the voice of the   supreme   pride   which speaks in

moi, à cette minute ? Tentai-je d'expliquer,
me   at   this   minute   ?   I attempted   of to explain

d'excuser par de trop subtiles et vaines raisons la
of to excuse by   of   too   subtle   and   vain   reasons   the

retombée de l'ange que j'aurais   pu   être, à
falling back   of   the angel that I would have been able to be   at

la croupissante, à l'immonde larve que je suis ?
the   stagnant   at   the unclean   larva that I   am   ?

Oh ! non ! je n'ai pas d'orgueil, je n'ai plus
Oh ! No ! I not have -not- of pride I not have more

d'orgueil ! Chaque fois que ce sentiment a voulu
of pride ! Each time that this feeling has wanted

pénétrer en moi, je n'ai eu, pour le chasser,
to enter in me I not have had for it to chase (away)

qu'à porter les yeux vers le ciel, vers ce
than to carry the eyes towards the sky towards this

gouffre épouvantant de l'infini, où je me sens
gulf frightening of the infinity where I myself feel

plus petit, plus inaperçu, plus infinitésimal que la
more little more unremarked more infinitesimal than the

diatomée perdue dans l'eau vaseuse des
diatom lost in the water muddy of the

citernes. Oh ! non, je le jure, je n'ai pas
tanks Oh ! No I it swear I not have -not-

d'orgueil.
of pride

Ce que j'ai voulu, c'est, en donnant à ces
This that I have wanted this is in giving to these

quelques souvenirs une forme animée et familière,
some few memories a shape animated and familiar

rendre plus sensible une des plus prodigieuses
make more sensible one of the most prodigious

tyrannies, une des plus ravalantes oppressions de
tyrannies one of the most debasing oppressions of

la vie – dont je n'ai pas été le seul à
-the- life – of which I not have -not- been the only (one) to

souffrir, hélas ! – : l'autorité paternelle. Car
suffer alas ! – : the authority paternal Because

tout le monde en a souffert, tout le monde
all the world of it has suffered all the world

porte en soi, dans les yeux, sur le front, sur la
carries in itself in the eyes on the face on the

nuque, sur toutes les parties du corps
neck on all the parts of the body

où   l'âme   se   révèle,   où   l'émotion   intérieure
where   the soul   itself reveals   where   the emotion   interior

afflue   en   lumières   attristées,   en   déformations
flows   in   lights   heartfelt   in   deformations

spéciales,   le   signe   caractéristique,   l'effrayant   coup
special   the   sign   characteristic   the frightening strike

de   pouce   de   cette   initiale,   de   cette   ineffaçable
of   thumb   of   this   initial   of   this   ineffaceable

éducation   de   la   famille.   Et   puis,   il   me   semble
education   of   the   family   And   then   it   me   appears

que   ma   plume,   qui   grince   sur   le   papier,   me
that   my   feather   which   creaks   on   the   paper   me

distrait   un   peu   de   l'effroi   de   ces   poutres,
distracts   a   bit   of   the fright   of   these   beams

d'où   quelque   chose   de   plus   lourd   que   le   ciel
from where some   thing   of   more   heavy   than   the   sky

du   jardin   pèse   sur   ma   tête.   Et   puis,   il   me
of the   garden   weighs   on   my   head   And   then   it   me

semble encore que les mots que je trace
appears still that the words that I trace

deviennent des êtres, des personnages vivants,
become of the beings of the characters living

des personnages qui remuent, qui parlent, qui
of the characters who stir who talk who

me parlent — oh ! concevez-vous la douceur de
to me talk — Oh ! do you conceive of the softness of
do you see

cette chose incompréhensible ! — qui me parlent
this thing incomprehensible ! — who to me talk

!...
!...

J'ai aimé mon père, j'ai aimé ma mère. Je les
I have loved my father I have loved my mother I them

ai aimés jusque dans leurs ridicules,
have loved until in their ridiculous (characteristics)

jusque dans leur malfaisance pour moi. Et, à
until in their maleficence for me And at

l'heure   où   je   confesse   cet   acte   de   foi,   depuis
the time   where   I   confess   this   act   of   faith   since

qu'ils   sont   tous   les   deux   là-bas,   sous   l'humble
that they   are   all   the   two   there down   under   the humble

pierre,   chairs   dissolues   et   vers   grouillants,   je   les
stone   flesh   dissolved   and   worms   seething   I   them

aime,   je   les   chéris   plus   encore,   je   les   aime   et
love   I   them   cherish   more   still   I   them   loves   and

je   les   chéris   de   tout   le   respect   que   j'ai   perdu.
I   them   cherish   with   all   the   respect   that   I have   lost

Je   ne   les   rends   responsables   ni   des   misères
I   not   them   render   responsable   neither   of the   miseries

qui   me   vinrent   d'eux,   ni   de   la   destinée
which   me   came   from them   nor   of   the   destiny

indicible   que   leur   parfaite   et   si   honnête
inexpressible   that   their   perfect   and   so   honest

inintelligence   m'imposa   comme   un
unintelligence   imposed on me   like   a

devoir. Ils ont été ce que sont tous les parents,
duty They have been this that are all the parents

et je ne puis oublier qu'eux-mêmes souffrirent,
and I not can forget that they themselves suffered

enfants, ce qu'ils m'ont fait souffrir. Legs fatal
children this that they me have made suffer Legacy fatal

que nous nous transmettons les uns aux autres,
that we ourselves pass on the ones to the others

avec une constante et inaltérable vertu.
with a constant and unalterable virtue

Toute la faute en est à la société qui n'a
All the fault of it is to the society who not has

rien trouvé de mieux pour légitimer ses actes
nothing found of better for to legitimate its acts

et consacrer, sans contrôle, son suprême
and devote without control its supreme

pouvoir, surtout pour maintenir l'homme servilisé,
power especially for to maintain the man servile

que d'instituer ce mécanisme admirable de
than of to institute this mechanism admirable of

crétinisation : la famille.
cretinisation : the family

Tout être, à peu près bien constitué, naît avec
All being to bit near well consisting is born with
almost

des facultés dominantes, des forces
-of- the faculties dominant -of the- forces
characteristics

individuelles, qui correspondent exactement à un
individual which match exactly to a

besoin ou à un agrément de la vie. Au lieu de
need or to an approval of the life At the place of
Instead

veiller à leur développement, dans un sens
keep watch to their development in a sense

normal, la famille a bien vite fait de les
normal the family has well quickly made of them

déprimer et de les anéantir. Elle ne produit
to depress and of them wreck She not produces
to suppress

que des déclassés, des révoltés, des
(other) than -of the- downgrades -of the- rebels -of the-

déséquilibrés, des malheureux, en les rejetant,
labile persons -of the- unhappies in them rejecting
unhappy people

avec un merveilleux instinct, hors de leur sein ;
with a wonderful instinct out of their breast ;

en leur imposant, de par son autorité légale, des
in them imposing of by its authority legal of the

goûts, des fonctions, des actions qui ne sont
likes of the functions of the actions which not are

pas les leurs, et qui deviennent, non plus une
-not- -the- theirs and which become no more a

joie, ce qu'ils devraient être, mais un intolérable
joy this that they should be but an intolerable

supplice. Combien rencontrez-vous, dans la vie, de
torment How much meet you in the life of

gens réellement adéquats à eux-mêmes ?
people actually adequate to themselves ?

J'avais un amour, une passion de la nature bien
I had   a   love   a   passion   of   the   nature   well

rares chez un enfant de mon âge. Et n'était-ce
rare   with   a   child   of   my   age   And   not was this

point là un signe d'élection ? Oh ! que je me
at all   there   a   sign   of election   ?   Oh !   that   I   myself
of choice

le suis souvent demandé ! Tout m'intéressait en
it   am   often   asked   !   All   interested me   in
have

elle, tout m'intriguait. Combien de fois suis-je
her   all   intrigued me   How much   of   time   am I
have I

resté, des heures entières, devant une fleur,
remained   of the   hours   whole   in front of   a   flower

cherchant, en d'obscurs et vagues tâtonnements,
searching   in   -of- obscure   and   vague   gropings

le secret, le mystère de sa vie ! J'observais les
the   secret   the   mystery   of   its   life   !   I observed   the

araignées, les fourmis, les abeilles,
spiders   the   ants   the   bees

les féeriques transformations des chenilles, avec
the fairy-like transformations of the caterpillars with

des joies profondes, traversées aussi de ces
of the joys deep traversed also of these

affreuses angoisses de ne pas savoir, de ne pas
dreadful fears of not -not- to know of not -not-

connaître. Souvent, j'adressais des questions à
to know Often I addressed -of the- questions to

mon père ; mais mon père n'y répondait
my father ; but my father not there answered
not them

jamais et me plaisantait toujours.
ever and me joked always
made fun of

— Quel drôle de type tu fais ! me disait-il...
— What funny of type you make ! me said he
a funny figure

Où vas-tu chercher tout ce que tu me racontes
Where go you seek all this that you me tell

?... Les abeilles, eh bien ! ce sont les femelles
?... The bees Eh well ! these are the females

des bourdons, comme les grenouilles sont les
of the bumblebees like the frogs are the

femelles des crapauds... Et elles piquent les
females of the toads And they sting the

enfants paresseux... Es-tu content, maintenant ?
children lazy Are you satisfied now ?

Quelquefois, il était plus bref.
Sometimes he was more Short

— Hé ! tu m'embêtes avec tes perpétuelles
— Hey! ! you bother me with your perpetual

interrogations !... Qu'est-ce que cela peut te faire
interrogations !... What is it that that can you make
do for you

?...
?...

Je n'avais ni livre, ni personne pour me guider.
I had neither book nor person for me to guide

Pourtant, rien ne me rebutait et c'était, je
However nothing not me discouraged and it was I

crois, une chose vraiment touchante que cette
believe a thing really touching -that- this

lutte d'un enfant contre la formidable et
fight of a child against the great and

incompréhensible nature.
incomprehensible nature

Un jour qu'on creusait un puits à la maison, je
One day that one dug a well at the house I

conçus, tout petit et ignorant que je fusse, la loi
conceived all little and ignorant that I was the law

physique qui détermina la découverte des puits
physical which determined the discovery of the wells

artésiens.
artesian

J'avais été souvent frappé, dans mes quotidiennes
I had been often struck in my daily

constatations, de ce phénomène de l'élévation des
findings of this phenomenon of the rise of the

liquides dans les vases se communiquant.
liquids in the vases themselves communicating

J'appliquai, par le raisonnement cette théorie
I applied by the reasoning this theory

innée et bien confuse encore dans mon esprit,
innately and well confused still in my mind

aux nappes d'eau souterraines, et je conçus, oui,
to the sheets of water underground and I designed yes

par une explosion de précoce génie, je conçus la
by an explosion of precocious genius I designed the

possibilité d'un jaillissement d'eau de source, au
possibility of a gushing of water of source at the
of spring water

moyen d'un forage, dans un endroit déterminé
means of a drilling in a place determined

du sol.
of the ground

Je fis part de cette découverte à mon père. Je
I made share of this discovery to my father I

la lui expliquai du mieux que je pus, avec un
it him explained of the best that I could with an

afflux de paroles et de gestes, qui ne m'était
influx of words and of gestures which not to me was

pas habituel.
-not- habitual

— Qu'est-ce que tu me chantes là ? s'écria
— What is it that you me sing there ? exclaimed

mon père... Mais c'est le puits artésien que tu
my father But this is the well artesian that you

as découvert, espèce de petite brute !
have discovered kind of little brute !

Et je vois encore le sourire ironique qui plissa
And I see still the smile ironic which narrowed

son visage glabre, et dont je fus tout humilié.
his face glabrous and of which I was all humiliated

— Je ne sais pas, balbutiai-je... Je te demande...
— I not know -not- I stammered I you request

— Mais, petite bourrique, il y a longtemps que
— But little donkey it there has long time that
it has been a

c'est découvert, les puits artésiens !... Ah ! ah ! ah
this is discovered the well artesian !... Ah ! Ah ! Ah

! Je parie que, demain, tu découvriras la lune !...
! I bet that tomorrow you discover the moon !...

Et mon père éclata de rire. Ce rire, comme
And my father broke out of laughter This laughter like
in

il me fit mal !
it me made bad !

Ma mère survint. Elle ne m'était pas indulgente
My mother appeared She not to me was -not- indulgent

non plus.
not more
either

— Tu ne sais pas, lui dit mon père... Nous avons
— You not know -not- him said my father We have

un grand homme pour fils ! Le petit vient de
a great man for (a) son ! The little (one) comes of

découvrir les puits artésiens !... ma parole
to discover the well artesian !... my word

d'honneur !
(of) honor !

— Oh ! l'imbécile ! glapit ma mère... Il ferait
— Oh ! the fool ! yelped my mother He would make

bien mieux d'apprendre son histoire sainte...
well better of to learn his history (of the) Saint

Ce fut au tour de mes sœurs qui accoururent,
This was -at- the turn of my sisters who rushed up
 It

avec leurs visages pointus et curieux.
with their faces sharp and curious

— Saluez votre frère, mesdemoiselles... C'est un
— Greet your brother misses This is a

grand inventeur !... Il vient de découvrir les puits
great inventor !... He comes of to discover the well

artésiens !
artesian !

Et mes sœurs, désagréables et méchants roquets,
And my sisters unpleasant and naughty pugs

jappèrent, et, grimaçant, et me tirant la langue :
yapped and grimacing and me pulling the tongue :

— Il ne sait quoi inventer pour être ridicule !...
— He not knows what to invent for be ridiculous !...

Bête, bête, bête !...
Animal animal animal !...

Puis enfin, les amis, les voisins, tout le pays,
Then finally the friends the neighbors all the country

surent tôt bien que j'avais découvert un moyen de
knew early well that I had discovered a means of

creuser les puits, comme on enfonce une cuiller
to dig the well like one inserts a spoon

dans un pot à beurre. Ce fut, autour de ma
in a pot to butter This was around of my
                        There

pauvre petite personne humiliée, un éclat de
poor little person humiliated an explosion of

rire méprisant, et des moqueries qui
laughter contemptuous and of the mockeries which

durèrent longtemps. Je sentis la déconsidération
lasted (a) long time I felt the disrespect

de toute une ville peser sur moi, comme si j'eusse
of all a town weigh on me like if I had

commis un crime.
committed a crime

Et je faillis mourir de honte.
And I failed to die of shame
      almost died

II

Je ne dépassai pas l'école primaire où,
I not surpassed -not- the school primary where
went farther than

d'ailleurs, je n'obtins aucun succès, je dois le
anyway I not obtained any success I must it

dire. Mon père avait déclaré à l'instituteur, en me
to say My father had declared to the teacher in me

confiant à lui, que j'étais excessivement borné,
confiding to him that I was excessively thick headed

et qu'il ne tirerait rien de moi. Celui-ci
and that he not would pull nothing (out) of me That one

s'en tint respectueusement à cette opinion,
himself of it held respectfully to this opinion

et n'essaya même pas, une seule fois, de se
and not tried even -not- a single time of himself

rendre compte de ce qu'il pouvait bien y avoir
to render account of this that it could well there have

derrière cette stupidité que m'octroyait, avec
behind this stupidity that me granted with

tant d'assurance, l'autorité paternelle. Et,
so much of assurance the authority paternal And

naturellement, cette opinion bien constatée et
naturally this opinion well recognized and

indiscrètement répandue, je devins le
indiscreetly spread on I became the

souffre-douleur de mes camarades, comme j'avais
suffer-pain of my comrades like I had
butt

été celui de ma famille.
been the one of my family

Il fut pourtant question, un moment, de m'envoyer
It was however question a moment of to send me

au collège ; mais réflexion faite, et toutes
to the college ; but reflection made and all
thought

raisons pesées, on décida que mon éducation était
reasons weighed one decided that my education was

suffisante ainsi.
sufficient   thus

— Il est bien trop bête, pour aller au collège
— He is well too animal for to go at the college
                        stupid

!... disait ma mère... Nous n'en aurions que
!... said my mother We not of it would have (other) than

 des ennuis.
of the annoyances

— Des mortifications !... appuyait mon père, qui
— Of the mortifications !... supported my father who
        embarrassments

aimait les grands mots.
loved the great words

— Oui ! Oui ! Qu'est-ce qu'il ferait au collège
— Yes ! Yes ! What is this that he would do at the college

?... Rien, parbleu !... Ce serait de l'argent perdu
?... Nothing egad !... This would be of the money lost

!
!

Mes sœurs consultées, car elles montraient, en
My sisters consulted because they showed in

toutes choses, un précoce bon sens, glapirent :
all things a precocious good sense yelped :

— Au collège !... Lui ?... Ah ! l'imbécile !...
— At the college !... Him ?... Ah ! the fool !...

D'un autre côté, on ne voulait pas me garder,
Of an other side one not wanted -not- me to keep

toute la journée, à la maison où j'étais une
all the day at the house where l was a

cause de perpétuel agacement, surtout depuis la
cause of perpetual annoyance especially since the

si malheureuse invention du puits artésien. Je
so unhappy invention of the well artesian I

voyais nettement, dans les huit regards de ma
saw clearly in the eight looks of my

famille, la crainte que je ne découvrisse quelque
family the fear that I not would discover some

chose   de   plus   extraordinaire   encore   ;   et,   pour
thing   of   more   extraordinary   still   ;   and   for

m'en   ôter   l'idée,   il   ne   se   passait   pas   de
me of it   to remove   the idea   it   not   itself   passed   -not-   of
there   a

jour   qu'on   ne   me   rappelât,   aigrement,   avec   de
day   that they   -not-   me   reminded   bitterly   with   of

lourdes   ironies,   et   de   persistantes   humiliations,   le
heavy   ironies   and   of   persistent   humiliations   the

souvenir   de   cette   ridicule   aventure.   Moi,   qui
memory   of   this   ridiculous   adventure   Me   who

n'avais   plus   le   droit,   sous   peine   de   dures
not had   more   the   right   under   pain   of   hard

réprimandes   ou   d'intolérables   moqueries,   de   faire
reprimands   or   of intolerable   mockeries   of   to make

un   geste,   ni   de   toucher   à   un   objet   ;   moi,
a   gesture   nor   of   to touch   -to-   an   object   ;   me

qu'on   rendait   responsable   de   ce   qu'il   advenait
that one   made   responsible   of   this   what it   became

de fâcheux, de la pluie, de la grêle, de la
of griefs of the rain of the hail of the

sécheresse, de la pourriture des fruits, j'étais
drought of the decay of the fruits I was

prêt à accepter, comme une délivrance, tout ce
ready to accept like a deliverance all this

que la fantaisie saugrenue de mes parents
that the fancy ridicule of my parents

pourrait leur suggérer, en vue de mon avenir,
could them suggest in sight of my future

comme ils disaient. De mon avenir !
like they said Of my future !

Il fut donc résolu que je travaillerais chez le
It was then decided that I would work with the

notaire comme « sous-saute-ruisseau », étrange et
notary like under-jump-stream strange and
deputy errand boy

nouvelle fonction que le tabellion n'hésita
new function that the scrivener not hesitated
official scribe

pas à créer, en considération de l'amitié qui
-not- to create in consideration of the friendship which

le liait à notre famille.
him bound to our family

— On verra plus tard ! conclut mon père...
— One will see more late ! concluded my father
            later

L'important, aujourd'hui, est de lui mettre le
The important (part) today is of him to put the

pied à l'étrier...
foot at the stirrup

Mes sœurs se marièrent à quelques mois
My sisters themselves married at some months

de distance, et peu après mon ordination dans
of distance and (a) bit after my ordination in

le notariat. Elles épousèrent des êtres vagues,
the notaries They married of the beings vague

étrangement stupides, dont l'un était receveur
strangely stupid of which the one was recipient

de l'enregistrement, et l'autre, je ne sais plus
of   the record   and the other I not know (any)more

quoi. Non, en vérité, je ne sais plus quoi.
what   No   in   truth   I not know (any)more what

À peine si je leur adressai la parole, et je les
At pain if I them addressed the word   and I them
It was barely that

traitai comme des passants.
treated him like   of the passersby

Quand ils eurent compris que je ne comptais
When they had understood that I not counted

pour rien dans la famille, ils me négligèrent
for nothing in the family they me neglected

totalement, me méprisèrent tous les deux pour ma
totally me despised all the two for my
both of them

faiblesse, pour mes façons solitaires et gauches,
weakness for my manners lonely and lefts
clumsy

pour tout ce qui n'était pas eux, en moi.
for all this which -not- was not them in me

C'étaient de grands gaillards, bruyants et
They were -of- tall fellows noisy and

vantards, ayant beaucoup vécu dans la lourde,
boasters having much lived in the heavy

dans l'asphyxiante bêtise des petits cafés de
in the asphyxiating stupity of the small cafes of

village. Ils y avaient appris, ils en avaient
(the) village They there had learned they of it had

gardé des gestes spéciaux et techniques. Par
guarded of the gestures special and techniques For
kept

exemple, quand ils marchaient, avançaient le
example when they moved advancing the

bras, saluaient, mangeaient, ils avaient toujours
arm saluted eating they had always

l'air de jouer au billard, de préparer des
the air of to play at the billiard table of to prepare of the

effets rétrogrades, importants et difficiles. Et,
effects retrogressive important and difficult And

naturellement, il leur était arrivé des aventures
naturally it them was arrived -of the- adventures
they had had

merveilleuses, de frissonnantes histoires, où ils
wonderful of chilling stories where they

s'étaient conduits en héros. Dans la famille
themselves were behaved in heroes In the family
as

et dans le pays, on les trouva excessivement
and in the country one them found excessively

distingués.
distinguished

— Sont-elles heureuses ! s'exclamait-on, en enviant
— Are they happy ! exclaimed people in envying
They're so fortunate

mes sœurs.
my sisters

Le receveur de l'enregistrement avait débuté,
The recipient of the record had started

comme fonctionnaire, dans un petit canton des
like official in a little Canton of the

Alpes. Il y avait chassé le chamois, ce
Alps He there had hunted the chamois this
Alpine goat antelopes

qui le rendait un personnage admirable, auréolé
which him rendered a character admirable aureole
gave

de légende et de mystère. Lorsqu'il racontait ses
of legend and of mystery When he told his

prouesses, il mimait avec des gestes
prowesses he mimed with -of the- gestures

formidables les gouffres noirs, les hautes cimes,
formidable the chasms black the high summits

les guides intrépides, et les chamois
the guides fearless and the chamois
Alpine goat antelopes

bondissants ; ma sœur, extasiée, atteignait les purs,
leaping ; my sister ecstatically reached the pure

les ivres, les infinis sommets de l'amour. Et
the drunk the endless peaks of -the- love And

qu'elle était laide, alors !
what she was ugly then !

L'autre   n'avait   pas   chassé   le   chamois,
The other   did not have   -not-   hunted   the   chamois
Alpine goat antelopes

mais   il   avait   sauté   des   barrières,   et   il   les
But   he   had   jumped   of the   barriers   and   he   them
over   fences

sautait   encore.   Il   les   sautait   avec   une   hardiesse,
jumped   still   He   them   jumped   with   a   boldness

une   souplesse   qui   faisaient   battre   le   cœur   de
a   flexibility   which   makes   beat   the   heart   of

mon   autre   sœur   comme   si   son   fiancé   eût   pris   une
my   other   sister   like   if   her   fiancé   had   taken   a

ville   d'assaut,   dispersé   des   armées,   conquis
city   by assault   scattered   -of the-   armies   conquered

des   peuples.   Le   dimanche,   à   la   promenade,
-of the-   peoples   The   Sunday   at   the   walk

tout   d'un   coup,   à   la   vue   d'une   barrière,   il
all   of a   blow   at   the   sight   of a   fence   he
sudden

interrompait   la   conversation,   prenait   son   élan,
interrupted   the   conversation   took   his   momentum

sautait   et   ressautait   la   barrière ;   puis,
jumped   and   jumped back (over)   the   fence   ;   then

revenant   près   de   nous,   il   nous   défiait   l'un
coming back   near   of   us   he   us   challenged   the one

après   l'autre :
after   the other :

— Faites-en   autant !
—   Do of it   as much !

Il   s'adressait   à   moi,   avec   une   insistance   qu'on
He   himself addressed   to   me   with   an   insistence   that one

trouvait   fort   spirituelle   et   d'un   goût   délicat.
found   very   spiritual   and   of a   taste   delicate

— Voyons ! Essayez ! faites-en   autant.
—   See   !   Try   !   Do of it   as much

Et   c'étaient   des   rires   moqueurs.
And   there were   -of the-   laughs   mockers

— Oh ! lui !... Il   ne   sait   rien   faire, lui !... Il
—   Oh   !   him   !...   He   not   knows   nothing   to do   him   !...   He

ne sait même pas courir... il ne sait même
not knows even -not- to run he not knows even

pas marcher !...
-not- to walk !...

Alors, jusqu'au soir, il fallait entendre le
Then until at the evening it was necessary to hear the

récit — telle une épopée — de toutes les barrières
story — such an epic — of all the barriers

qu'il avait franchies, des barrières hautes
that he had crossed -of the- barriers high

comme des maisons, comme des chênes, comme
like of the houses like of the oak trees like

des montagnes — et des barrières vertes,
of the mountains — and of the barriers green

rouges, bleues, blanches, et des murs, et des
red blue white and of the walls and of the

haies... En racontant, il tendait le jarret, le
hedges In recounting he stretched the hock it

raidissait, le faisait jouer, fier de ses muscles...
stiffened the made play proud of his muscles

Mon autre sœur défaillait d'amour, elle aussi,
My other sister fainted of love she also

emportée, par l'héroïsme de cet incomparable
carried along by the heroism of this incomparable

jarret, dans un rêve de joies sublimes et
hock in a dream of joys sublime and

redoutables.
redoubtable

On les trouva, une après-midi, sur le banc de
One them found one afternoon on the bench of

la tonnelle, ma sœur à demi pâmée entre les
the arbor my sister at half swooning between the

jarrets de son fiancé. Il fallut avancer le
hocks of her fiancé It was necessary to move forward the

mariage.
marriage

Et je me souviens de scènes horribles, de
And I myself remember of scenes horrible -of-

répugnantes et horribles scènes, le soir, dans
disgusting and horrible scenes the evening in

le salon, à la lueur terne de la lampe, qui
the salon at the gleam dull of the lamp which

éclairait, d'une lueur tragique, d'une lueur de
lit with a gleam tragical with a gleam of

crime, presque, ces étranges visages, ces visages
crime almost these strange faces these faces

de fous, ces visages de morts.
of crazy people these faces of dead people

La mère du receveur de l'enregistrement vint
The mother of the recipient of the record came

une fois pour régler les conditions du contrat
one time for to adjust the conditions of the contract
wedding

et l'ordonnance du trousseau. Elle voulait
and the arranging of the trousseau She wanted
wedding household gifts

tout avoir et ne rien donner, disputant sur
all   to have   and   not   nothing   to give   competing   on

chaque article, âprement ; son visage se ridait
each   article   bitterly   ;   her   face   itself   wrinkled

de plis amers ; elle coulait sur ma sœur des
with   folds   bitter   ;   she   flowed   on   my   sister   of the

regards aigus, des regards de haine, et elle
looks   sharp   of the   looks   of   hatred   and   she

répétait sans cesse :
repeated   without   stop   :

— Ah ! mais non !... On n'avait pas dit ça !...
—   Ah   !   but   no   !...   One   did not have   -not-   said   that   !...

Il n'a jamais été question de ça !... Un châle
It   not has   ever   been   question   of   that   !...   A   shawl

de l'Inde !... Mais c'est de la folie !... Nous ne
of   the India   !...   But   this is   of   the   madness   !...   We   not

sommes pas des princes du sang,
are   -not-   of the   princes   of the   blood

nous autres !...
we others !...

Mon père qui avait cédé sur beaucoup de points
My father who had ceded on many -of- points

s'emporta, lorsque la vieille dame eut contesté
himself took away / got angry when the old lady had disputed

le châle de l'Inde.
the shawl of the India

— Nous ne sommes pas des princes du sang,
— We not are -not- of the princes of the blood

c'est possible ! dit-il avec une dignité... Mais nous
this is possible ! said he with a dignity But we

sommes des gens convenables, des gens
are of the people suitable of the people

honorables... Nous avons une situation, un rang...
honorable We have a situation / position a rank

Le châle de l'Inde a été promis... Vous
The shawl of the India has been promised You

44

donnerez le châle de l'Inde...
give the shawl of the India

Et d'une, voix nette, catégorique, il ajouta :
And of one voice clear categorical he added :

— Je l'exige... J'ai pu faire des sacrifices
— I it demand I have been able to make -of the- sacrifices

au bonheur de ces enfants... Mais ça !... je
to the happiness of these children But that !... I

l'exige !
it require !

Il se leva, se promena dans le salon, les
He himself raised himself walked in the salon the

mains croisées derrière le dos, les doigts agités
hands crossed behind the back the fingers agitated

par un mouvement de colère... Il y eut un
by a movement of anger It there had a
                                         There was

moment de dramatique silence.
moment of dramatic silence

Ma mère était très pâle ; ma sœur avait les yeux
My mother was very pale ; my sister had the eyes

gonflés, la gorge serrée. Le receveur de
inflated the throat closed The recipient of

l'enregistrement ne pensait plus aux
the record not thought (any)more to the
of the

chamois et fixait un regard embarrassé sur
chamois and fixed a look embarrassed on
Alpine goat antelopes

une chromo-lithographie, pendue au mur, en
a chromo-lithography hung on the wall in

face de lui. La vieille dame reprit :
face of him The old lady continued :

— Et ça nous avancera bien, tous, que cette
— And that us will advance well all that this
will do

petite ait un châle de l'Inde, si elle n'a rien
little one has a shawl of the India if she not has nothing

à manger.
to eat

— Ma fille !... rien à manger ? interrompit mon
— My girl !... nothing to eat ? interrupted my

père, qui se plaça tout droit et presque
father who himself placed all straight and almost

menaçant devant la vieille dame, dont le
threatening in front of the old lady of which the

visage se plissa ignoblement... Et pour qui me
face itself narrowed vilely And for who me

prenez-vous, Madame ?
do you take Madam ?

Mais elle s'obstina :
But she persisted :

— Un châle de l'Inde !... Je vous demande un
— A shawl of the India !... I you request a

peu !... Savez-vous ce que cela coûte, seulement ?
little !... Know you this what that costs only ?

47

— Je   n'ai   pas   à le savoir, Madame... Je   n'ai
— I   not have   -not- to it to know   Madam   I   not have

à savoir que ceci : une chose promise est une
to know than this : a thing promised is a

chose promise !
thing promised !

Ma mère de plus en plus pâle, intervint :
My mother of more in more pale intervened :

— Madame !... C'est l'habitude !... Un trousseau est
— Madam !... This is the habit !... A trousseau is

un trousseau !... Nous n'avons pas demandé de
a trousseau !... We -not- have not asked of

dentelles, bien que dans notre position, nous
laces well that in our position we

eussions pu exiger aussi un châle de
had been able to require also a shawl of

dentelles... Mais, le châle de l'Inde !... Voyons,
laces But the shawl of the India !... See

Madame, les filles d'épiciers en ont !... Ça ne
Madam the girls of grocers them have !... That not

serait pas un mariage sérieux !
would be -not- a marriage serious !

La vieille dame, qui était à bout d'arguments,
The old lady who was at end of arguments

frappa sur le guéridon, de sa main sèche.
knocked on the pedestal table with her hand dry

— Eh bien, non ! cria-t-elle, je ne donnerai pas
— Eh well no ! she cried out I not will give -not-

de châle de l'Inde... Si vous voulez un châle de
of shawl of the India If you want a shawl of

l'Inde, vous le paierez... A-t-on vu ?... C'est mon
the India you it will pay Have they seen ?... This is my
                                     Do you see

dernier mot !
last word !

Ma sœur dont les yeux étaient pleins de larmes,
My sister of which the eyes were full of tears

n'y   put   tenir   davantage.   Elle   sanglota,
not there   could   keep   (any)more   She   sobbed
not them

s'étouffa   dans   son   mouchoir,   hoquetant
herself choked   in   his   tissue   hiccupping

douloureusement, et si déplorablement laide que
painfully   and so   deplorably   ugly   that

je détournai d'elle mes yeux pour ne pas la voir.
I turned away of her my eyes for not -not- her to see

— Je n'en veux pas... du châle... de l'Inde...
— I not of it want -not- of the shawl of the India

gémissait-elle... Je veux me marier !... Je veux
she moaned   I want myself marry !... I want
to marry myself

me marier !
myself marry !

— Ma fille ! s'écria mon père.
— My girl ! exclaimed my father

— Ma pauvre enfant ! s'écria ma mère.
— My poor child ! exclaimed my mother

— Mademoiselle ! Mademoiselle ! s'écria le

receveur de l'enregistrement dont les bras

allaient et venaient comme s'ils eussent poussé

une longue queue sur un long billard.

Entre ses hoquets, ses sanglots, ma sœur suppliait

d'une voix cassée, d'une voix étouffée dans

l'humide paquet de son mouchoir :

— Je veux me marier !... Je veux me marier !

On l'entraîna dans sa chambre... Elle se laissait

conduire, ainsi qu'une chose inerte, répétant :
lead thus than one thing inert repeating :

— Je veux me marier... Je veux me marier...
— I want myself to marry I want myself to marry

Ce fut sur moi que se passa la colère de la
This was on me that itself passed the anger of the
It

famille. Mon père m'apercevant, tout à coup, me
family My father seeing me all at blow me
of a sudden

gifla et me poussa hors du salon, furieux.
slapped and me pushed out of the salon furious

— Et pourquoi es-tu ici ?... Qui t'a prié de
— And why Are you here ?... Who your prayed of
asked

venir ici ?... C'est de ta faute, ce qui
to come here ?... This is -of- your fault this which

arrive... Allons, va-t'en...
arrives Go go from here

Ainsi, d'ailleurs, se terminaient toutes les scènes.
Thus anyway itself ended all the scenes

Ma sœur se maria, sans châle de l'Inde ;
My sister herself married without shawl of the India ;

puis elle partit. Mon autre sœur se maria
then she left My other sister herself married

également, sans châle de l'Inde, puis elle partit...
equally without shawl of the India then she left

Et je n'entendis plus le glapissement de mes
And I not heard (any)more the yelping of my

sœurs.
sisters

Un silence envahit la maison. Mon père devint
A silence invaded the house My father became

très triste. Ma mère pleura, ne sachant plus
very sad My mother cried not knowing (any)more

que faire de ses longues journées. Et les serins
what to do with her long days And the canaries

de mes sœurs, dans leur cage abandonnée,
of my sisters in their cage abandoned

périrent, l'un après l'autre.
perished   the one   after   the other

Moi, je copiais des rôles chez le notaire, et je
Me   I   was copying   of the   roles   with   the   notary   and   I

regardais, d'un œil amusé, le défilé, en blouses
watched   with an   eye   amused   the   parade   in   blouses

bleues et en sabots, de toutes les passions, de
blue   and   in   clogs   of   all   the   passions   of

tous les crimes, de tous les meurtres que souffle
all   the   crimes   of   all   the   murders   that   breath

à l'âme des hommes l'âme homicide de la
to   the soul   of the   men   the soul   homicidal   of   the

Terre.
Earth

III

Je suis né avec le don fatal de sentir vivement,
I   am born with the gift fatal of to feel   strongly

de sentir jusqu'à la douleur, jusqu'au ridicule. Dès
of to feel up to the   pain   up to the ridiculous From

ma toute petite enfance je donnais, au moindre
my all little childhood I gave   at the   least

objet, à la moindre chose inerte, des formes
object to the least   thing inert of the forms

supravivantes, en mouvement et en pensée.
super-living   in movement and in thought
living

J'accumulais sur mon père, ma mère, mes sœurs,
I accumulated on my father my mother my sisters
from

des observations irrespectueuses et désolantes,
-of the- comments   disrespectful   and distressing

qui n'étaient pas de mon âge. D'autres eussent
which not were -not- of my age -Of- others had
for

tiré parti, plus tard, de ces qualités
pulled part / more late / of these qualities
left behind / later

exceptionnelles ; moi, je ne fis qu'en souffrir,
exceptional ; me I not made what of it suffer

et elles me furent, toute la vie, un embarras.
and they me were all the life an embarrassment

En même temps que cette sensibilité suraiguisée
In (the) same time as this sensitivity over-sharp

par l'ironie, j'avais une grande timidité, si grande
by the irony I had a large timidity so great

que je n'osais parler à qui que ce fût, pas
that I not dared to speak to who(ever) that this was not

même à mon père, qui m'en avait ôté toute
even to my father who me of it had removed all

envie, pas même au chien de mon père, le
envy not even to the dog of my father the

vieux Tom, lequel participait à la répulsion et à
old Tom who participated to the repulsion and to

la crainte dont j'englobais toute la famille,
the fear of which I encompassed all the family

car il affectait, lui aussi, de ne pas me
because he affected him also of not -not- me
      pretended

comprendre.
to understand

Ne pas être compris par un chien, n'est-ce point
Not -not- to be understood by a dog not is this point

le dernier mot de la détresse morale ? J'avais
the last word of the distress moral ? I had

donc fini par garder tout pour moi et en moi.
then finished by to keep all for me and in me
                                   myself   myself

À peine répondais-je aux questions qui m'étaient
At pain i answered to the questions which me were
   Barely

adressées. Bien souvent, sans raison, je n'y
addressed Well often without reason I not there
                                              not them

répondais que par des larmes.
answered (other) than by -of the- tears

Vraiment, je n'ai pas eu de chance. J'ai
Really I not have -not- had of fortune I have

grandi dans un milieu tout à fait défavorable
grown in an environment all at fact unfavorable

au développement de mes instincts et de mes
to the development of my instincts and of my

sentiments. Et je n'ai pu aimer personne,
feelings And I not have been able to love anyone

moi qui, par nature, étais organisé pour aimer
me who by nature was organized for to love

trop et trop de gens. Dans l'impossibilité
too (much) and too (many) of people In the impossibility

où j'étais d'éprouver de l'amour pour quelqu'un,
where I was of to prove of the love for someone

je le simulai, et je crus écouler ainsi le
I it feigned and I believe flow out thus the

trop-plein des tendresses qui bouillonnaient en
too-full of the tendresses which seethed in

moi. En dépit de ma timidité, je jouais la comédie
me In spite of my timidity I played the comedy

des effusions, des enthousiasmes ; j'eus des
of the effusions of the enthusiasms ; i had of the

folies d'embrassements qui me divertirent et me
follies of embarrassments which me entertained and me

soulagèrent un moment. Mais l'onanisme n'est pas
relieved a moment But the onanism not is -not-

l'amour. Loin d'éteindre les ardeurs génésiques,
-the- love Far from to switch off the ardor reproductive

il les surexcite et les fait dévier vers
it them overexcites and them makes deviate towards

l'inassouvi.
the unfulfilled

*
**
*
**

Quelques mois après le mariage de mes sœurs,
Some months after the marriage of my sisters

j'eus une fièvre typhoïde, qui se compliqua de
I had a fever typhoid which itself complicated with

méningite, et, par miracle, j'en guéris.
meningitis and by miracle I of it healed

La maladie liquéfia, en quelque sorte, mon
The disease liquefied in some kind my

cerveau. Dès que je bougeais la tête, il me
brain From that I shifted the head it me

semblait qu'un liquide se balançait, entre les
seemed that a liquid itself balanced between the

parois de mon crâne, comme dans une bouteille
walls of my skull like in a bottle

remuée. Toutes mes facultés subirent un temps
stirred All my faculties suffered a time

d'arrêt. Je vécus dans le vide, suspendu et
stop I lived in the emptiness suspended and

bercé dans l'infini, sans aucun point de contact
rocked · in the infinity without any point of contact

avec la terre. Je demeurai longtemps en un état
with the earth I remained (a) long time in a state

d'engourdissement physique et de sommeil
of numbness physical and of sleep

intellectuel, qui était doux et profond comme la
intellectual which was sweet and deep like the

mort. Sur l'avis du médecin, mes parents,
death On the opinion of the docter my parents

inquiets et honteux de moi, me laissèrent
worried and shameful of me me left

tranquille, et décidèrent que je ne retournerais
quiet and decided that I not would return

pas chez le notaire.
-not- with the notary

Ce fut pour moi une époque d'absolu bonheur,
This was for me a time of absolute happiness

et dont je n'ai véritablement conscience
and of which I not have truly consciousness

qu'aujourd'hui. Durant plus d'une année, je savourai
today During more than a year I savored

– incomparables délices de maintenant – la joie
– incomparable delights of now – the joy

immense, l'immense paix de ne penser à rien.
immense the immense peace of not to think to nothing
of

Étendu sur une chaise-longue, les yeux toujours
Stretched out on a chaise longue the eyes always

fermés à la lumière, j'avais la sensation du
closed to the light I had the feeling of the

repos éternel, dans un cercueil. Mais la chair
rest eternal in a coffin But the flesh

repousse vite aux blessures des enfants ; les
regrows quickly to the wounds of the children ; the

os fracturés se ressoudent
bone fractured themselves solder back (together)

d'eux-mêmes ; les jeunes organes se
by themselves ; the young organs themselves

remettent promptement des secousses qui les
put back promptly from the shakes which them

ont ébranlés ; la vie a bien vite fait de
have disturbed ; the life has well quickly made of

rompre les obstacles qui arrêtent un moment le
to break the obstacles which stop a moment the

torrent de ses sèves. Je repris des forces, et,
torrent of its saps I resumed -of- the forces and

avec les forces revenues, peu à peu, je redevins
with the forces returned bit by bit I became again

la proie de l'éducation familiale, avec tout ce
the prey of the education domestic with all this

qu'elle comporte de déformations sentimentales, de
that she carries of deformations sentimental of

lésions irréductibles et d'extravagantes vanités.
injury irreducible and of extravagant vanities

Alors, tous les jours, à toutes les minutes,
Then all the days at all the minutes

j'entendis mes parents, à propos de choses que
I heard my parents to proposals of things that

j'avais faites ou que je n'avais pas faites, dire sur
I had done or that I not had -not- done say on

un ton, tantôt irrité, tantôt compatissant : «
a tone sometimes irritated sometimes compassionate :

C'est désolant !... Il ne comprend rien !... Il ne
This is sad !... He not understands nothing !... He not

comprendra jamais rien... Quel affreux malheur
will understand ever nothing What awful misfortune

pour nous que cette méningite ! » Et ils
for us -that- this meningitis ! And they

regardaient avec effroi, mais sans oser me les
watched with fright but without to dare me them

reprocher — car c'étaient d'honnêtes gens,
blame — because they were -of- honest people

selon la loi, — les morceaux que je dévorais
according to the law — the pieces that I devoured

avidement, dans le silence des repas, dont ils
greedily in the silence of the meal for which they

savaient très bien qu'ils ne seraient pas payés.
knew very well that they not would be -not- paid

Loin que ma sensibilité eût été diminuée par
Far (from) that my sensitivity had been decreased by

le mal qui avait si intimement atteint mes
the disease which had so intimately reached my

moelles, elle se développa encore, s'exagéra
marrow she itself developed still itself exaggerated
even more

jusqu'à devenir une sorte de trépidation nerveuse.
until to become a kind of tremor nervous

Quand mon père, avec une insouciance de
When my father with a carelessness of

perroquet, me demandait : « As-tu bien dormi,
parrot me asked : Have you well slept

cette nuit ? », je sanglotais à perdre la
this night ? I sobbed to lose the

respiration, à m'étouffer. De quoi, mon père, qui
breathing to myself smother Of what my father who

était un homme pratique, s'étonnait grandement.
was a man practical was astonished greatly

Ce mutisme éternel, coupé de temps à autre par
This mutism eternal cut from time to other by time

ces inexplicables larmes, ressemblait à un
these inexplicable tears resembled to an

incurable abrutissement, et ma famille ne pouvait
incurable brutalization dumbification and my family not could

s'y faire. Tout me fut une souffrance. Je
itself there make Everything to me was a suffering I

recherchais je ne sais quoi dans la prunelle des
looking I not know what in the sloe eye of the

hommes, aux calices des fleurs, aux formes si
men to the chalices of the flowers to the forms so

changeantes, si multiples de la vie, et je
changing so multiple of the life and I

gémissais de n'y rien trouver qui
moaned of not there nothing to find which

correspondît au vague, obscur et angoissant
corresponded to the vague obscure and scary

besoin d'aimer qui emplissait mon cœur, gonflait
need of to love which filled my heart swelled

mes veines, tendait toute ma chair et toute mon
my veins stretched all my flesh and all my

âme vers d'inétreignables étreintes et
soul towards of unembracable hugs and

d'impossibles caresses.
of impossible caresses

Une nuit que je ne dormais pas, j'ouvris la
One night that I not slept -not- i opened the

fenêtre de ma chambre et, m'accoudant sur la
window of my room and leaning me on the

barre d'appui, je regardai le ciel, au-dessus du
bar of support I looked at the sky above of the

jardin noyé d'ombre. Le ciel était mauve, de ce
garden drowned of shade The sky was mauve of this
with darkness purple

mauve si tendre, si pur, si doucement irradiant,
mauve so tender so pure so softly radiating
purple

et, dans ce mauve, des millions d'étoiles
and in this mauve -of the- millions of stars
purple

brillaient. Pour la première fois, j'eus conscience
shone For the first time I had consciousness

de cette immensité formidable, de cette immensité
of this immensity great of this immensity

couleur de fleur, que j'essayais de sonder —
color of flower that I tried of to fathom —

est-ce comique ? — avec de pauvres petits
Is this comical ? — with -of- poor small

regards d'enfant, et j'en fus tout écrasé. J'eus la
looks of child and I of it was all crushed I had the

terreur de ces étoiles si muettes, dont le
terror of these stars so silent of which the

clignotement recule encore, sans l'éclairer jamais,
blink recedes still without to enlighten ever

l'affolant mystère de l'incommensurable.
the maddening mystery of the immeasurable

Qu'étais-je, moi, si petit, parmi ces mondes ? De
What was I me so little among these worlds ? Of

qui donc étais-je né ? Et pourquoi ? Où donc
who then was I born ? And why ? Where then

allais-je, vile fibre, imperceptible atome perdu dans
went I vile fiber imperceptible atom lost in

ce calme tourbillon des impénétrables harmonies
this calm whirlwind of the impenetrable harmonies

? Et qu'étaient mon père, ma mère, mes sœurs,
? And what were my father my mother my sisters

nos voisins, nos amis, les passants, toute cette
our neighbors our friends the passersby all this

poussière vivante, toute cette
dust alive all this

minuscule troupe d'insectes emportée par on ne
tiny band of insects carried along by one not

sait quoi, vers on ne sait où ? Je n'avais
knows what towards one not knows where ? I not had

pas lu Pascal — je n'avais rien lu encore —
-not- read Pascal — I not had nothing read still —

et, quand, plus tard, cette phrase que je cite de
and when more late this sentence that I cite from

mémoire, me tomba sous les yeux : « Je ne sais
memory me fell under the eyes : I not know

qui m'a mis au monde, ni ce que c'est que
who me has put at the world nor this what this is that

le monde, ni que moi-même. Je suis dans une
the world nor that my self I am in an

ignorance terrible de toutes ces choses », je
ignorance terrible of all these things I

tressaillis de joie et de douleur, de voir exprimés
flinched of joy and of pain of to see expressed

si nettement, si complètement, les sentiments qui
so clearly so completely the feelings which

m'avaient agité cette nuit-là.
me had agitated this night there

Toute cette nuit-là, je restai appuyé contre la
All this night there I remained leaned against the

fenêtre ouverte, sans un mouvement, le regard
window opened without a movement the look

perdu dans l'épouvante du ciel mauve, et la
lost in the terror of the sky mauve and the
purple

gorge si serrée que les sanglots dont était pleine
throat so closed that the sobs of which was full

ma poitrine ne pouvaient s'en échapper et
my chest not could themselves of it escape and

me suffoquaient. Mais le matin, enfin, reparut.
me suffocated But the morning finally reappeared

L'aube se leva et, avec elle, la
The dawn itself raised and with her the

vie, qui dissipe les songes de mort et qui
life which dissipates the dreams of death and which

couvre de bruits familiers le silence oppressant
covers with noises familiar the silence oppressive

de l'infini. Des portes s'ouvrirent, des volets
of the infinity -Of the- doors itself opened -of the- shutters

claquèrent sur les murs, une pie s'envola d'une
slammed on the walls a magpie flew with a

touffe de troènes, les chats, bondissant dans
tuft of privet the cats leaping in
{plant}

l'herbe humide, rentrèrent de leurs chasses
the grass wet returned from their hunting

nocturnes. Je vis la cuisinière qui balaya le
nightly I saw the cook who swept the
{female}

seuil de notre maison ; je vis ma mère
threshold of our house ; I saw my mother

descendre dans le jardin, étendre sur la pelouse
go down in the garden spread on the lawn

des linges grossiers et des carrés de laine
of the cloths coarse and of the squares of wool

brune. De la fenêtre où je l'observais, elle était
brown From the window where I her observed she was

douloureusement hideuse. Sa silhouette revêche
painfully hideous Her silhouette surly

chagrinait le réveil si frais, si pur du matin ;
distressed the waking up so fresh so pure of the morning ;

les fleurettes du gazon s'offensaient de son
the flowers of the lawn themselves took offense of her

sale bonnet de nuit et de sa camisole fripée. Son
dirty cap of night and of her blouse wrinkled Her

jupon noir, mal attaché aux hanches, clapotait
petticoat black badly attached to the hips sloshed

sur d'infâmes savates qui traînaient dans l'herbe,
on -of- infamous slippers which dragged in the grass

pareilles à
similar to

de   répugnants   crapauds.   Elle   avait   une   nuque
-of-   loathsome   toads   She   had   a   neck

méchante,   un   profil   dur,   un   crâne   obstiné.   Rien
malicious   a   profile   hard   a   skull   obstinated   Nothing

de   maternel   n'avait   dû   jamais   faire   frissonner
of   maternal   did not have   had to   ever   make   shiver

ce   corps   déformé.   Tout   d'abord   sa   vue   m'irrita
this   body   deformed   All   of first   her   sight   me irritated

comme   une   tache   sur   une   belle   étoffe   de   soie
like   a   stain   on   a   beautiful   fabric   of   silk

claire.   Et   puis,   j'eus   une   immense   pitié   d'elle,   qui
clear   And   then   i had   an   immense   pity   of her   which

me   fit   fondre   en   larmes.   J'aurais   voulu,   à
me   made   melt   in   tears   I would have   wanted   at

force   de   baisers   et   de   caresses,   faire   pénétrer
force   of   kisses   and   of   caresses   to make   penetrate

dans   ce   crâne,   sous   ce   bonnet,   un   peu   de   la
in   this   skull   under   this   cap   a   bit   of   the

clarté de ce virginal matin. Je descendis au
light of this virginal morning I descended to the

jardin, et, courant vers ma mère, je me jetai
garden and running towards my mother I me threw

dans ses bras :
in her arm :

— Maman !... maman !... maman !... implorai-je...
— Mama !... Mama !... Mama !... I implored

Pourquoi ne regardes-tu pas les étoiles, la nuit ?
Why not do you watch -not- the stars the night ?

Elle poussa un cri, effrayée de ma voix, de mon
She emitted a cry scared of my voice of my

regard, de mes larmes, et, s'arrachant à mes
look of my tears and herself tearing to my
from

embrassements, elle s'enfuit.
embraces she herself fled
ran away

Ce jour-là, j'accompagnai mon père aux obsèques
This day there I accompanied my father to the obsequies
funeral

d'un vieux fermier que je connaissais à peine. Au
of an old farmer that I knew at pain At the
barely

cimetière, durant le défilé devant la fosse, je fus
graveyard during the parade in front of the pit I was

pris d'une étrange tristesse. Quittant la foule des
taken by a strange sadness Leaving the crowd of the

gens qui se bousculaient et se
people who themselves jostled and themselves

disputaient l'aspersoir, je courus à travers
vied it to sprinkle (with sand) I ran -at- through

le cimetière. Je me heurtais aux tombes et
the graveyard I myself bumped into to the tombs and

pleurais à fendre l'âme d'un fossoyeur. Mon père
cried at to split the soul of a gravedigger My father
enough to split

me rejoignit.
me joined again

— En bien ? Qu'est-ce que tu as ?... Pourquoi
— In well ? What is it that you have ?... Why

pleures-tu ? Pourquoi t'en vas-tu ? Es-tu
are you crying ? Why you of it go you ? Are you

malade ?
sick ?

— Je ne sais pas, gémis-je... Je ne peux pas...
— I not know -not- i moaned I not can -not-

Mon père me prit par la main, et me ramena
My father me took by the hand and me brought back

à la maison.
to the house

— Voyons, raisonna-t-il... Tu ne le connaissais
— See he reasoned You not him knew

pas, le père Julien ?
-not- the father Julian ?

— Non !
— No !

— Par conséquent, tu ne l'aimais pas ?
— By consequence you not loved him -not- ?

— Non.
— No

— Alors, qu'est-ce qui te prend ?... Pourquoi
— Then what is this which you takes ?... Why
got into you

pleurer ?
cry ?

— Je ne sais pas...
— I not know -not-
don't

— Regarde-moi, voyons !... Je le connaissais, moi,
— Look at me see !... I him knew me

le père Julien... C'était un homme qui payait
the father Julian It was a man who paid

régulièrement ses fermages... Sa mort me laisse
regularly his rents His death me leaves

dans un grand embarras. Peut-être que je ne
in a large embarrassment Maybe that I not

retrouverai jamais un fermier pareil à lui... Eh bien
will find back ever a farmer similar to him Eh well

!... Est-ce que je pleure, moi ?
!... Is this that I cry me ?

Et, après un silence, d'une voix plus sévère, mon
And after a silence with a voice more severe my

père ajouta :
father added :

— Ce n'est pas bien, ce que tu fais là. Tu ne
— This not is -not- well this that you do there You not

sais quoi inventer pour me mortifier... Je ne suis
know what to invent for me to mortify I not am

pas content, du tout ! Ce matin, tu dis a ta
-not- satisfied of the all ! This morning you say to your
at

mère, on ne sait quoi... Maintenant, tu pleures
mother one not knows what Now you cry

à propos de rien... Si tu continues, je
at proposals nothing If you continue I

ne t'emmènerai   plus   jamais avec moi...
not   you will take (any)more   ever   with   me

81

IV

Autrefois, habitait avec nous une cousine de ma
(The) other time lived in with us a cousin of my

mère. Elle était fort difficile à vivre et si
mother She was very difficult to live (with) and so

singulière, « si originale », si déséquilibrée en ses
singular so original so unbalanced in her
strange

actions, qu'on « ne savait jamais à quoi s'en
actions that one not knew ever to what oneself of it

tenir avec elle ». Tantôt elle m'accablait de
to keep with her Sometimes she overwhelmed me with
to behave

tendresses et de cadeaux, et, la minute d'après,
tendernesses and with gifts and the minute -of- after

elle me battait sans raison. Pif ! paf ! des
she me beat without reason Bop ! bam ! of the

claques, à propos de rien.
slaps to aim of nothing
about

Souvent, elle me pinçait le bras, sournoisement,
Often she me pinched the arm slyly

quand je passais près d'elle dans les corridors, ou
when I passed near of her in the corridors or

bien, si je la frôlais dans l'escalier, elle
well if I her brushed against in the stairs she

m'embrassait avec furie. Et je ne savais jamais à
hugged me with fury And I not knew ever to
{now: kissed me}

quoi attribuer ses effusions ou ses coups,
what to attribute her effusions or her blows

également désobligeants.
equally derogatory

En tout ce qu'elle faisait, elle semblait obéir aux
In all this what she did she seemed to obey to the

suggestions d'une folie incompréhensible.
suggestions with a madness incomprehensible

Quelquefois, elle restait enfermée des journées
Sometimes she remained locked up of the days
for

entières, dans sa chambre, triste, pleurant ; le
whole in her room sad weeping ; the

lendemain, prise de gaietés bruyantes et de
following day taken of gaieties noisy and of

dévorantes activités, elle chantait. Je l'ai vue
consuming activities she sung I her have seen

remuer, dans le bûcher, d'énormes bûches qu'elle
stir in the (wood) pyre enormous logs that she

déplaçait sans utilité, et, dans le jardin, piocher
displaced without utility and in the garden plow
moved tools

la terre, plus ardente au travail qu'un terrassier.
the earth more burning at the work than a navvy
fiery road worker

Elle était fort laide, si laide que personne jamais
She was very ugly so ugly that no one ever

ne l'avait demandée en mariage, malgré ses six
not her had asked in marriage in spite of her six

mille livres de rente. On pensait dans la
thousand pounds of annuity They thought in the

famille qu'elle souffrait beaucoup de son état de
family that she suffered much from her state of

vieille fille, et que c'était là la cause de ses
old girl, and that it was there the cause of her
spinster

actes désordonnés. La figure couperosée, la peau
acts disorderly The figure blotched the skin

sèche et comme brûlée, et soulevée en squames
dried and like burned and raised in scales

cendreuses par du feu intérieur, les cheveux
cindery by of the fire interior the hairs
hair

rares et courts, très maigre, un peu voûtée, ma
scarce and short very thin a bit vaulted my
stooping

pauvre cousine était vraiment bien désagréable à
poor cousin was really well unpleasant to

voir. Ses subites tendresses me gênaient plus
see Her sudden tendernesses me bothered more

encore que ses colères imprévues. Elle avait, en
still than her anger unexpected She had in

m'embrassant furieusement, des gestes si durs,
kissing me furiously of the gestures so hard

des mouvements si brusques, que je préférais
of the movements so sudden that I preferred

encore qu'elle me pinçât le bras.
still that she me pinched the arm

Un jour, à la suite d'une discussion futile et
A day at the following of a discussion futile and
after a

qui, tout de suite, dégénéra en querelle, elle
which all of following degenerated in quarrel she
immediately

partit. Elle partit sans nous dire où elle allait.
left She left without us to say where she went

Elle partit avec ses malles et ses meubles, et si
She left with her trunks and her furniture and so

colère qu'elle ne voulut même pas nous
angry that she not wanted even -not- us

embrasser. Et, pendant quatre ans, nous
embrace And during four years we

n'entendîmes plus parler d'elle. On finit, à
not heard (any)more speak of her One ended at

force de recherches, par savoir qu'elle vivait seule
force of researches by to know that she lived alone

dans une petite bourgade de Normandie, près de
in a little village of Normandy near of

la mer. Au dire des gens qui nous
the sea At the to say of the people who us
According to the

renseignèrent, il y avait bien du mystère dans
informed it there had well of the mystery in
there was

sa maison. Il y venait, presque tous les
her house -It- there came almost all the

dimanches, un adjudant de cuirassiers, en garnison
Sundays an adjutant of cuirassiers in garrison

dans la ville voisine.
in the city neighboring

— Ça ne m'étonne pas, disait ma mère... Ça
— That not astonishes me -not- said my mother That

la   tracassait   !...   C'était   visible   que   ça   la
her   worried   !...   It was   visible   that   that   her

tracassait...
   worried

Elle   ne   pouvait   se   faire   à   l'idée   de   perdre   un
She   not   could   herself   make   to   the idea   of   to lose   a
                             get used

héritage   qu'elle   avait   toujours   considéré   comme
heritage   that she   had   always   considered   like

assuré.   Cet   adjudant   hantait   sans   cesse   son
assured   This   adjutant   haunted   without   stop   her

esprit   et   la   poursuivait   jusque   dans   ses   rêves.
mind   and   her   persecuted   until   in   her   dreams

Très   souvent,   dans   un   silence,   tout   à   coup,   elle
Very   often   in   a   silence   all   to   strike   she
                             all of a sudden

disait,   sans   s'adresser   particulièrement   à   l'un
said   without   herself address   particularly   at   the one
                                     any

de   nous :
of   us   :

— Pourvu qu'elle ne fasse pas la bêtise de
— Provided that she not makes -not- the stupity of

l'épouser !
him marry !

Elle écrivit plusieurs lettres affectueuses à ma
She wrote several letters affectionate to my

cousine, qui ne daigna pas répondre.
cousin who not deigned -not- to answer

Quelque temps après, nous apprîmes qu'à
Some time after we learned than at

l'adjudant de cuirassiers, parti pour une garnison
the adjutant of cuirassiers left for a garrison

lointaine, avait succédé un adjudant de dragons,
distant had succeeded an adjutant of dragoons

lequel fut à son tour remplacé par un autre
which was at his turn replaced by an other

adjudant de je ne sais plus quelle arme.
adjutant of I not know more what weapon

Décidément, **ma** **pauvre** **cousine** **ne** **montait** **pas**
Definitely my poor cousin not climbed -not-

en **grade.**
in grade

Et, **un** **soir** **d'hiver,** **je** **me** **souviens,** **un** **soir**
And one evening of winter I myself remember an evening

de **pluie** **battante,** **l'omnibus** **de** **l'hôtel** **s'arrêta**
of rain beating the horse-tram of the hotel stopped

devant **la** **grille,** **chargé** **de** **malles** **et** **de**
in front of the gate loaded with trunks and with

paquets. **Ma** **cousine** **en** **descendit,** **secoua** **la**
packages My cousin of it descended shook the

sonnette **furieusement,** **et** **au** **milieu** **des**
(the) bell furiously and at the middle of the

ébahissements, **des** **exclamations** **de** **toute** **la**
astonishments of the exclamations of all the

maisonnée **mise** **en** **branle,** **elle** **entra,** **vive** **et**
household put in motion she entered lively and

nerveuse   comme   autrefois,   mais   encore   plus
nervous   like   (the) other time But   still   more
                       before

maigre,   plus   voûtée,   plus   couperosée.   Elle   dit
thin   more   vaulted   more   blotched   She   said
                 stooped

simplement :
simply   :

— C'est moi !... Je reviens... Voilà...
— This is me !... I   come back See there

— As-tu   tes   meubles ? demanda ma mère...
— Have you your furniture ?   asked   my   mother

— Oui, j'ai   mes meubles ! répondit ma cousine...
— Yes I have my   furniture ! answered my   cousin

 J'ai   tout... Je reviens...   Voilà !
I have   all   I   come back See there !

Et   la vie recommença comme par le passé...
And the life   began again   like   by   the   past
                                          in

Ma cousine m'avait trouvé changé et grandi.
My   cousin   had me   found   changed and grown
                thought I was

— Mais tu es très joli... Tu es un homme... Un
— But you are very pretty You are a man A

vrai homme, maintenant... Approche un peu que je
true man now Approach a bit that I
                                                      so

te voie mieux.
you see better

Elle m'examina, me tâta les bras, les mollets.
She examined me me patted the arm the calves

— Un amour d'homme, un amour de petit homme
— A love of man a love of little man
               lovely man   lovely

! conclut-elle, en m'embrassant à me briser la
! she concludes in me hugging at me break the
                  {now: kissing me} almost breaking

poitrine, contre sa sèche et dure carcasse de
chest against her dried and hard carcass of

vieille folle.
old crazy woman

Bientôt, son affection comme ses méchancetés
Soon her affection like her wickedness

prirent une forme exaspérée qui m'épouvanta.
took a shape exasperated which terrified me
exasperating

Quelquefois, après le déjeuner, elle m'entraînait
Sometimes after the lunch she dragged me

en courant, ainsi qu'une petite fille, vers le
while running just that a little girl towards the
like a

fond du jardin. Il y avait là une salle de
back of the garden It there had there a room of
There was

verdure, et dans cette salle, un banc. Nous
greenery and in this room a bench We

nous asseyions sur le banc sans rien nous
ourselves sat on the bench without nothing us

dire. Ma cousine ramassait sur le sol une
to say My cousin gathered on the ground a

brindille morte et la mâchait avec rage. Sa
twig dead and it chewed with rage Her

couperose s'avivait de tons plus rouges ;
rosacea was heightened of tones more red ;
{chronic condition}

sa   peau   écailleuse   se   bandait   sur   l'arc   tendu
her   skin   scaly   itself   strained   on   the bow   extended
the curve

de   ses   joues   et,   dans   ses   yeux   congestionnés,   et
of   her   cheeks   and   in   her   eyes   congested   and

virant   comme   des   barques   sur   des   remous,
turning   like   of the   boats   on   of the   swirls

d'étranges   lueurs   brillaient.
of strange   lights   shone

— Pourquoi   ne   me   dis-tu   rien   ?... demandait-elle,
—   Why   not   me   you say   nothing   ?...   asked she

après   quelques   minutes   de   silence   gênant.
after   some   minutes   of   silence   embarrassing

— Mais,   ma   cousine...
—   But   my   cousin

— Est-ce   que   je   te   fais   peur   ?...
—   Is it   that   I   you   make   fear   ?...

— Mais non, ma cousine...
— But no my cousin

— Oh ! regarde !... comme tu es mal cravaté !...
— Oh ! look !... how you are badly tied !...
have messed up your tie

Quel petit désordre tu fais !
What little disorder you make !
look like

Et, m'attirant près d'elle, elle arrangeait le nœud
And pulling me near of her she arranged the knot

de ma cravate avec des gestes vifs et
of my tie with -of the- gestures lively and

heurtés... Je sentais les os de ses doigts se
clashed I felt the bone of her fingers itself
clashing

frotter à ma gorge ; son souffle fade, d'une
scrub at my throat ; her breath bland with a

chaleur aigre, offusquait mes narines. J'aurais
heat sour offended my nostrils I would have

bien voulu m'en aller, – non que je
well wanted me of it to go – not that I

soupçonnasse un danger quelconque, mais toutes

suspected a danger any but all

ces pratiques m'étaient intolérables.

these practices me were intolerable

actions

— Voyons !... parle donc !... Es-tu bête !... Es-tu

— See !... speak then !... Are you animal !... Are you

dumb

empoté !

clumsy !

Et, tout à coup, comme poussée par un ressort,

And all to strike like pushed by a spring

all of a sudden

elle se levait, piétinait la terre avec impatience

she herself raised trampled the earth with impatience

et me lançait un vigoureux soufflet.

and me launched a vigorous bellows

slap in the face

— Tiens ! attrape !... Tu es un sot !... tu es une

— Hold ! catch !... You are a fool !... you are a

petite bête... une vilaine petite bête...

little animal an unpleasant little animal

Et elle partait vivement, étouffant dans sa course
And she left strongly stifling in her run

le bruit d'un sanglot...
the noise of a sob

Un après-midi, nous étions assis sur le banc,
An afternoon we were seated on the bench

dans la salle de verdure, ma cousine et moi.
in the room of greenery my cousin and me

Il faisait très chaud ; de lourdes nuées d'orage
It made very warm ; -of- heavy clouds stormy
was

s'amoncelaient dans l'Ouest.
were gathering in the west

— Pourquoi regardes-tu Mariette avec des yeux
— Why do you watch Mariette with -of the- eyes

comme ça ?... me demanda brusquement ma
like that ?... me asked abruptly my

cousine.
cousin

Mariette était une petite bonne que nous avions
Mariette was a little good (girl) that we had

alors, et dont j'aimais, il est vrai, sans y
then and of which I loved it is true without there
who

mêler de coupables pensées, la peau fraîche et
to mix of guilty thoughts the skin fresh and

blanche, et la nuque blonde.
white and the neck blonde

— Mais, je ne regarde pas Mariette, répondis-je,
— But I not watch -not- Mariette answered I

étonné de cette question.
surprised by this question

— Je te dis que tu la regardes... Je ne veux
— I you say that you her look at I not want

pas que tu la regardes... C'est très mal... Je le
-not- that you her look at This is very bad I it

dirai à ta mère...
will say to your mother

— Je t'assure, ma cousine, insistai-je...
— I assure you my cousin I insisted

Je n'eus pas le temps d'achever ma phrase...
I had not -not- the time of to complete my sentence

Enlacé, étouffé, broyé par mille bras, on
Entwined choked crushed by (a) thousand arms one

eût dit, dévoré par mille bouches, je
had said devoured by (a) thousand mouths I
would have

sentis l'approche de quelque chose d'horrible,
felt the approach of some thing -of- horrible

d'inconnu ; puis l'enveloppement sur moi,
unknown ; then the wrapping on me

l'enroulement sur tous mes membres, d'une bête
the winding on all my members of an animal

atroce. Je me débattis violemment... Je repoussai
atrocious I myself struggled violently I pushed

la bête qui semblait multiplier ses tentacules à
the animal who seemed multiply her tentacles at

chaque seconde ; je la repoussai des dents,
each second ; I her pushed back with the teeth

des ongles, des coudes, de toute la force
with the fingernails with the elbows of all the force

décuplée par l'horreur.
increased tenfold by the horror

— Non... non... je ne veux pas... criai-je... Ma
— No no I not want -not- I cried My
don't want to

cousine, je ne veux pas... je ne veux pas...
cousin I not want -not- I not want -not-
don't want to don't want to

— Mais tais-toi donc !... tais-toi, petit
— But silence-yourself then !... silence-yourself little
be quiet be quiet

monstre ! râlait ma cousine dont les lèvres
monster ! groaned my cousin of which the lips

roulaient sur mes lèvres.
rolled on my lips

— Non ! cessez, ma cousine... cessez... ou
— No ! stop my cousin stop or

j'appelle maman...
    I call   Mama

L'étreinte mollit, quitta ma poitrine, mes jambes...
The embrace abated   left   my   chest   my   legs

Les tentacules rentrèrent dans leur gaine... Mes
The   tentacles   pulled back   in   their   sheath   My

lèvres délivrées purent aspirer une bouffée d'air
 lips   freed   could   inhale   a   puff   of air

frais... Et, entre les branches, je vis ma cousine
 fresh   And between the   branches   I saw my   cousin

fuyant, à travers les plates-bandes, vers la
 fleeing -at- through the   flat bands   towards the
                                causeways

maison...
    house

Je n'osai rentrer que le soir, à l'heure
 I not dared to enter (other) than the evening at the time

du dîner, inquiet, à l'idée de revoir ma
of the dinner worried at the idea of to see again my

cousine.
cousin

— Ta cousine est partie, me dit mon père, le
— Your cousin is / has part / left me said my father the

front soucieux. Elle a eu une discussion avec
face concerned She has had a discussion / argument with

Mariette. Je la connais. Cette fois, elle ne
Mariette I her know This time she not

reviendra plus. C'est embêtant !
will come back (any)more This is annoying !

Le dîner fut silencieux et morose. Chacun
The dinner was silent and morose Each

regardait la place vide de six mille livres de
watched the place empty of six thousand pounds of

rentes.
annuities

Nous n'avons jamais revu ma cousine.
We -not- have ever seen again my cousin

Et   voilà   comment je connus ce que c'était que
And see there   how   I known this that it was that

l'amour !
the love   !

V

Je veux maintenant conter le seul amour qui
I   want   now   tell (about) the only love which

ait, un instant, illuminé ma vie, comme disent les
has a moment illuminated my life like say the

poètes. Et l'on verra de quelle lumière.
poets And -it- one will see of what light

J'avais grandi. Un duvet roux dessinait, sur mes
I had grown A down red drew on my

lèvres, l'arc d'une moustache naissante à peine,
lips the bow / the curve of a mustache nascent / growing at / barely pain

et, quoique je fusse à l'époque difficile, peu
and though I was at the time difficult little

harmonieuse, de la croissance, avec de trop
harmonious from the growth with -of- too

grands bras et de trop grandes jambes qui
long arms and -of- too long legs which

rendaient ma démarche dégingandée et un peu
rendered my step ungainly and a bit
made

comique, avec un buste trop court et de trop
comical with a chest too short and -of- too

gros os, sous la peau, — imperfections
big bones under the skin — imperfections

plastiques qu'accentuaient singulièrement les
plastics accentuated by singularly the
very much

prodigieux costumes, retaillés dans les défroques
prodigious dresses recut in the castoffs

paternelles, dont ma mère m'affublait, — je
paternal with which my mother me decked out — I
of my father

n'étais pas laid. Au contraire. Mes yeux avaient
was not -not- ugly At the contrary My eyes had

une grande douceur, un éclat triste et profond,
a large softness a shine sad and deep

fort touchant, par quoi se tempérait de
very touching by what itself tempered with
because of which

grâce   rêveuse   le   ridicule   que   me   valaient   les
(a) grace   dreamy   the   ridicule   that   me   earned   the

ajustements   économiques   haussés,   par   une   fantaisie
adjustments   economically   raised   by   a   fancy

de   coupe   presque   géniale,   jusqu'au   rire   grinçant
of   cut   almost   genius   up to the   laugh   grating

de   la   caricature.   J'ai   conservé   longtemps   une
of   the   caricature   I have   preserved   long   a

photographie   faite,   un   jour   de   prodigalité,   par   un
photography   made   one   day   of   prodigality   by   an

artiste   forain,   de   passage   chez   nous.   Elle   me
artist   showman   of   passage   with   us   She   me
visiting   It

représentait   à   l'âge   dont   je   parle,   et   sous   ce
represented   at   the age   of which   I   speak   and   under   this

déguisement,   que   je   considère   presque   comme   un
disguise   that   I   considered   almost   like   a

crime   de   lèse-enfance.   En   dépit   de   toutes   les
crime   of   wrong childhood   In   spite   of   all   the

mélancolies, en dépit de tous les souvenirs de
melancholies in spite of all the memories of

haine que cette ancienne image remuait en moi, il
hatred that this ancient image moved in me it

m'arrivait souvent de la regarder et il ne m'était
happens to me often of it to look at and it not me was

point difficile d'y reconnaître, sous
at all difficult to there recognize under

l'accoutrement baroque, certaines beautés qui
the trappings baroque certain beauties which
beautiful things

avaient le don de m'émouvoir jusqu'aux larmes.
had the gift of to move me up to the tears

Jusqu'au jour où, dans la salle de verdure, ma
Up to the day where in the room of greenery my

pauvre et douloureuse cousine avait tenté sur
poor and pained cousin had tempted on

ma personne ce demi-viol que j'ai raconté,
my person this half rape that I have told (about)

j'étais demeuré parfaitement chaste. La puberté
l was / I had — remained — perfectly — chaste — The — puberty

s'établissait en moi, lente et calme, sans
established itself — in — me — slow — and — calm — without

violences, sans secousses, sans troubles
violence — without — shakes — without — problems

d'aucune sorte. À ce phénomène physiologique
of any — kind — To — this — phenomenon — physiological

correspondait une plus grande expansion de tout
fit — a — more — large — expansion — of — all

mon être dans la nature, voilà tout. J'aimais
my — being — in — the — nature — see there — all — I loved

davantage, j'aimais d'un inexprimable amour, les
more — I loved — with an — inexpressible — love — the

fleurs, les arbres, les nuages, les étoiles du
flowers — the — trees — the — clouds — the — stars — of the

firmament nocturne ; j'aurais voulu épouser
firmament — nocturne — ; — I would have — wanted — to marry

toutes les formes ambiantes, me fondre dans
all the forms ambient me melt in

toutes les musiques. C'étaient, on le voit, des
all the musics They were one it sees -of the-

sensations très vagues, dans lesquelles aucun désir
sensations very vague in which any desire

ne se précisait. Mais de ce jour où, si
not itself stated But from this day where so

brutalement et si incomplètement, je dois le dire,
brutally and so incompletely I must it say

me fut révélé le mystère de l'acte sexuel, je
me was revealed the mystery of the act sexual I

n'eus plus une minute de tranquillité physique et
not had more a minute of tranquility physical and

morale. D'étranges hantises survinrent qui
moral -Of- strange hauntings appeared which

secouèrent ma chair réveillée et peuplèrent
shook my flesh woken up and peopled
filled

d'images brûlantes mes rêves, d'où la pureté
with images burning my dreams from where the purity

s'envola.
itself flew off

Les femmes que je n'avais pas considérées, alors,
The women that I not had -not- considered then

autrement que les hommes, et dont le contact
otherwise than the men and of which the contact

me laissait insensible, je les regardai davantage,
me let insensitive I them looked at more

avec des persistances étonnées, avec des
with -of- the persistence astonished with -of- the

doutes et de fatigantes curiosités. Je regardai
doubts and -of- exhausting curiosities I looked at
curiosity

leurs yeux, leurs lèvres, leurs mains, cherchant ce
their eyes their lips their hands searching this

qu'ils pouvaient contenir de
that they could contain of

significations nouvelles. Je regardai les plis de
meanings news I looked at the folds of
new meanings

leurs corsages, ouverts sur les nuques et sur les
their corsages open on the necks and on the

gorges, et les dévêtant par la pensée j'essayai,
throats and them undressing by the thought I tried

au moyen de comparaisons insuffisantes, de
at the means of comparison inadequate of

reconstituer la ligne des corps, la courbe des
to reconstruct the line of the body the curve of the

hanches, la rondeur du ventre, la floraison
hips the roundness of the belly the flowering
bloom

somptueuse des poitrines, et tout ce que
sumptuous of the breasts and all this that
splendid

j'ignorais de leurs formes voilées, de tous leurs
I did not know of their forms veiled of all their

organes interdits. Rien que de les frôler
organs prohibited Nothing (other) than of them to graze

en passant, cela me faisait courir dans les veines
in   passing   that   me   made   run   in   the   veins

un sang plus chaud, accélérait, quelquefois, jusqu'au
a   blood   more   warm   accelerated   sometimes   up to the

galop furieux, les battements de mon cœur.
gallop   furious   the   beats   of   my   heart

Je n'avais d'autres indications que celles, si furtives,
I   not had   -of- other   indications   than   those   so   stealthy

si rapides, si grimaçantes, de vue et de toucher,
so   quick   so   grimacing   of   sight   and   of   touch

acquises dans la lutte mémorable avec ma cousine
acquired   in   the   fight   memorable   with   my   cousin

; d'un autre côté, je n'avais jamais rien lu,
;   from an   other   side   I   not had   ever   nothing   read

car on me cachait tous les livres, de peur
because   they   (to) me   hid   all   the   books   (out) of   fear

qu'ils ne me pervertissent ; je
that they   -not-   me   (would) pervert   ;   I

n'avais, non plus, jamais vu une seule image de
not had · no · more · ever · seen · a · single · image · of

nudité, car les tableaux, les gravures, qui
nudity · because · the · scenes · the · engravings · which

ornaient les murs de la maison, ne reproduisaient
decorated · the · walls · of · the · house · not · reproduced

que des chiens, des fruits, des oiseaux, un
than · -of the- · dogs · -of the- · fruits · -of the- · birds · a

moulin au bord d'une rivière, des saints et
mill · at the · edge · of a · river · -of the- · Saints · and

des bonnes Vierges. Ma vie avait été
-of- the · good · Virgin (Mary) · My · life · had · been

préservée de tout contact avec des camarades,
preserved · from · all · contact · with · -of the- · comrades

dont je n'avais pu recevoir de confidences,
of which · I · not had · been able · to receive · -of- · confidences

ni aucun éclaircissement sur des questions qui
nor · any · clarification · on · -of the- · questions · which

113

ne me préoccupaient pas, d'ailleurs. J'acceptais,
not me concerned -not- anyway I accepted

avec une bonne grâce passive, que les enfants
with a good grace passive that the children

naquissent spontanément, dans les jardins, sous les
were born spontaneously in the gardens under the

choux. Les oiseaux sur les branches, au
cabbages The birds on the branches at the

printemps, les coqs dans la basse-cour, les
spring the roosters in the low-court the
yard for fowl

chiens rencontrés, dans les rues, en d'étranges
dogs encountered in the streets in of strange

postures, les insectes accouplés dans l'herbe, rien,
postures the insects mated in the grass nothing

dans ce rapprochement incessant des formes
in this reconciliation unceasing of the forms

vivantes dans lesquelles je vivais, n'avait pu
alive in which I lived not had been able

troubler l'impassible sérénité de mon âme,
to trouble the impassive serenity of my soul

ignorante et pure comme une petite étoile du
ignorant and pure like a little star of the / in the

ciel. Et voilà que, maintenant, pour avoir été
sky And see there that now for to have been

effleuré par les mains et par la bouche d'une
scratched by the hands and by the mouth of a

femme laide et vieille, pour avoir senti sur ma
woman ugly and old for to have felt on my

peau la peau eczémateuse d'une femelle en folie,
skin the skin with eczema of a female in madness

je m'épuisais en de continuelles imaginations,
I myself weary in -of- continual imaginations

dont l'impudeur ingénue et la naïveté
of which the shamelessness ingenuous and the naivete

luxurieuse devaient s'effacer – ah ! si
luxurious must effaces itself / disappear – Ah ! so

douloureusement ! – devant la réalité.
painfully ! – in front of -the- reality

Le pays manquait de jolies filles et de femmes
The country missed -of- pretty girls and -of- women

convenables à l'expérience que je voulais tenter.
suitable to the experience that I wanted to try

Elles étaient toutes vulgaires ou repoussantes, ou
They were all vulgar or repulsive or

si grossières de paroles et de gestes qu'il me
so rough of words and of gestures that it me

suffisait de leur parler pour les fuir.
suffised of them to talk to for (from) them to flee
was enough

Pourtant, bien des fois, à la nuit tombante, je
However well of the time at the night falling I
often

rôdai autour de la demeure d'une ignoble
prowled around of the abode of a despicable

créature, presque toujours ivre, et qui, pour
creature almost always drunk and who for

quelques   verres   d'eau-de-vie   et   pour   deux
some   glasses   of water spirits   and   for   two

sous,   se   livrait   aux   terrassiers.
sous   herself   gave over   to the   navvies
{old french coins}   road workers

Une   seule   me   plut.   Brune   de   cheveux   et   de
One   only   me   pleased   Brown   of   hairs   and   of
hair

peau   bronzée,   les   reins   souples   et   les   yeux
skin   tanned   the   sides   flexible   and   the   eyes

ardents,   elle   exhalait,   comme   une   fleur   sauvage,
fiery   she   exhaled   like   a   flower   wild

l'odeur   d'une   forte   et   puissante   jeunesse.   Chose
the smell   of a   strong   and   powerful   youth   Thing

rare   chez   nous,   elle   avait   des   dents   très
rare   with   us   she   had   -of the-   teeth   very

blanches,   et   une   bouche   très   rouge,   gonflée   d'une
white   and   a   mouth   very   red   inflated   with a

pulpe   humide   et   généreuse.   Tous   les   jours,   vers
pulp   wet   and   generous   All   the   days   towards
softness

midi, un paquet de linge en équilibre sur sa tête,
noon a package of linen in balance on her head

elle allait au lavoir. Le col nu, les manches
she went to the washhouse The neck nude the sleeves

retroussées jusqu'au coude, la mince étoffe de sa
rolled back up to the elbow the thin fabric of her

jupe bien collée sur ses cuisses, et toute sa
skirt well stuck on her thighs and all her

chevelure sombre et mate parsemée d'écume
hair dark and matt studded of scum

savoureuse, elle travaillait comme un homme et
tasty she worked like a man and

chantait comme un oiseau. Tous les jours, moi
sang like a bird All the days me

aussi, je me rendais au lavoir, aux heures
also I myself rendered to -the- washhouse at the hours

où j'étais sûr de la rencontrer. Mais comme elle
where I was sure of her to encounter But like she

n'était jamais seule, et que je redoutais les
not was ever alone and that I feared the

railleries des hardies commères, ses compagnes, je
taunts of the bold gossips her companions I
gossiping ladies

n'osai pas lui parler, ni même une seule fois
not dared -not- (to) her speak nor even a single time

l'aborder. D'ailleurs, ma famille, intriguée par ces
her address Anyway my family intrigued by these

sorties fréquentes, qui ne m'étaient pas
exits frequent which not (for) me were -not-

habituelles, m'ayant surveillé, me confina
usual me having watched me confined

sévèrement à la maison.
severely at the house

C'est alors que je songeai à Mariette, notre petite
It is then that I thought at Mariette our little

bonne, à qui ma cousine m'avait si injustement
good to who my cousin me had so unfairly

et si prophétiquement accusé de prodiguer mes
and so prophetically accused of to lavish my

attentions et mes désirs. Elle était vraiment
attentions and my desires She was really

charmante, cette Mariette, et je me reprochai
charming this Mariette and I myself reproached

de m'en apercevoir pour la première fois. Toute
of me of it to notice for the first time All

blonde et fraîche, d'une fraîcheur irradiante de
blonde and fresh with a freshness radiating of

fleur, le buste flexible, les hanches rondes et
(a) flower the chest flexible the hips rounds and

pleines comme un bulbe de lis, les yeux bleus
full like a bulb of (a) lily the eyes blue

étonnés et languides, elle m'apparut soudain,
astonished and languid she to me appeared suddenly

malgré ses rudes vêtements de paysanne et
in spite of her rough clothes of peasant woman and

ses lourds sabots, elle m'apparut pareille à une
her heavy clogs she to me appeared similar to a

petite fée ou à une petite reine. Cette vision
little fairy or to a little queen This vision

illumina mon âme d'une éblouissante lumière.
lit my soul with a dazzling light

Depuis qu'elle était à la maison, à peine si je
Since that she was at the house to pain if I
(it was) barely

lui avais adressé deux ou trois fois la parole.
her had addressed two or three times the word

D'être toujours rebuté et toujours, sous peine
Of to be always put off and always under pain

d'intolérables moqueries, condamné au silence,
of intolerable mockeries condemned to the silence

cela rend peu communicatif.
that makes little communicative
not very

— Est-il possible que je ne l'aie jamais vue !
— Is it possible that I not her have ever seen !

me	disais-je	avec	de	grands	regrets...	Moi	qui
myself	said I	with	-of-	great	regrets	Me	who

vivais	près	d'elle	!...	Ô	Mariette	!...	Mariette	!...
lived	near	of her	!...	Oh	Mariette	!...	Mariette	!...

ai-je	pu	être	aussi	longtemps	aveugle	?	Ai-je
have I	been able	to be	so such	(a) long time	blind	?	Have I

pu,	pendant	tant	de	mois,	mépriser	un
been able	during	so much	of	months	to despise	a

pareil	trésor	?
similar	treasure	?

Je	disais	«	trésor	»,	parole	d'honneur	!	sans
I	said		treasure		word	of honor	!	without

avoir	jamais	lu	un	livre	d'amour	;	tout	le
to have	ever	read	a	book	of love	;	all	the

vocabulaire	amoureux,	tout	le	dictionnaire	des
vocabulary	loving of a lover	all the whole	the	dictionary	of the

tendresses	bêtes	et	des	élans	ridicules	me	venait
tendernesses	animals daft	and	of the	spirits airs	ridiculous	me	came

spontanément   à   l'esprit.   Et   pourtant,   je   n'étais
spontaneously   to   the mind   And   however   I   was not

point amoureux   au   sens poétique de   ce   mot. Je
at all   in love   at the   sense   poetic   of   this   word   I

ne   rêvais   ni   dévouements surhumains,   ni
not   dreamed of   neither   devotions   superhuman   nor

sacrifices   extra-terrestres,   ni   de   parcourir   avec
sacrifices   out of this world   nor   of   to roam   with

elle, parmi les vols d'anges, les espaces célestes
her   among   the   flights   of angels   the   spaces   heavenly

et   les   hyperlyriques   régions   où   les   poètes
and   the   hyper lirical   areas   where   the   poets

conduisent   leurs   incorporelles   amantes.   Je
lead   their   intangible   lovers   I

n'éprouvais   pas   l'ivresse   mystique   de
did not experience   -not-   the intoxication   mystical   of

mourir et le besoin de transmuer mon corps en
to die   and the   need   of   to transmute   my   body   in

âme
(the) soul

de colombe ou de cygne. Non, ce que je voulais,
of (a) dove or of (a) swan No this that I wanted

c'était me jeter sur Mariette, comme ma cousine
it was me to throw on Mariette like my cousin

s'était jetée sur moi ; c'était surtout d'arracher,
herself was thrown on me ; it was especially -of- to tear
herself had

de mes doigts griffus, ces voiles de grossière
of my fingers clawed these sails of coarse

indienne qui s'interposaient entre elle et
Indian (cloth) which interposed themselves between her and

mon désir de la connaître toute... C'était de
my desire of her to know wholly It was of

jouir de sa splendeur nue !
to enjoy of her splendor nude !
nude splendor

L'amour m'avait rendu hardi. Et puis, Mariette
The love me had rendered bold And then Mariette

n'était pas, pour moi, comme eût été une autre
not was -not- for me like had been an other

femme. Elle était notre domestique soumise et
woman She was our servant submitted and

respectueuse. J'avais sur elle ma part d'autorité, et,
respectful I had on her my share of authority and

si peu établi qu'il fût, le prestige du maître.
so little established that it was the prestige of the master

Je ne quittai plus la cuisine, aux heures où
I not left (any)more the kitchen at the hours where

j'avais chance de ne pas être surpris par mes
I had fortune of not -not- to be surprised by my

parents. Et le moment ne tarda pas à venir
parents And the moment not delayed -not- to come

où, après une courte et molle lutte, après des
where after a short and soft fight after of the

: « Finissez donc, monsieur Georges ! » timides
: Stop then Mr. Georges ! timid

et langoureux, Mariette se donna à
and languoureux, Mariette herself gave to
     languorous
     lacking vitality

moi, sur une vieille chaise, près de la table,
me on an old chair near -of- the table

entre un vase de terre où trempaient des
between a vase of earth where soaked -of the-
clay

morceaux de morue et un poulet qu'elle venait
pieces of cod and a chicken that she came

d'éventrer.
of to eviscerate

VI

Ce fut une révolution complète de mes
This was a revolution complete of my

sentiments, et, par conséquent, de mon existence.
feelings and by consequence of my existence

À l'inverse de ce que les poètes disent de
At the reverse of this that the poets say of

l'influence « sublimatoire » de l'amour, l'amour tua
the influence sublimatory of the love the love killed

en moi toute poésie. Je ne vis plus les choses
in me all poetry I not saw (any)more the things

à travers le voile miséricordieux et charmant
-at- through the veil merciful and charming

de l'illusion, et la réalité dégradante m'apparut,
of the illusion and the reality demeaning to me appeared

qui n'est pas, d'ailleurs, plus réelle
which not is -not- anyway more real

que le rêve, puisque ce que nous voyons autour
than the dream since this that we see around

de nous, c'est nous-mêmes, et que les extériorités
of us this is ourselves and that the externalities

de la nature ne sont pas autre chose que des
of -the- nature not are -not- other thing that of the

états plastiques, en projection, de notre intelligence
states plastic in projection of our intelligence

et de notre sensibilité.
and of our sensitivity

Ce qui causa la déchéance de mon idéal ancien,
This which caused the decline of my ideal former

était-ce le lieu vulgaire où la prodige s'était
was this the place vulgar where the prodigy itself was / itself had

accompli ? Était-ce l'objet même de ma
accomplished ? Was it the subject same of my

passion, ce pauvre petit être insignifiant et
passion this poor little being insignificant and

borné,　　inconscient　et　passif,　qui　ne　pouvait
thick headed　unconscious　and　passive　who　not　could

favoriser　par　son　prestige　et　maintenir　par　sa
promote　by　her　pride　and　maintain　by　her

beauté　cette　exaltation　de　l'univers　en　moi,　par
beauty　this　exaltation　of　the universe　in　me　through

quoi　ma　vie　s'était　toujours　embellie　jusque
what　my　life　itself was　always　embellished　until
　　　itself had　　　made more beautiful

dans　la　médiocrité　et　la　souffrance,　et　s'était
in　the　mediocrity　and　the　pain　and　itself was
　　　　　　　itself had

aussi　dramatisée　jusque　dans　la　somnolence　et
also　dramatized　up to　in　the　drowsiness　and
so

l'abrutissement ?　Je　ne　sais...　Non, en　vérité, je
brutishness　?　I　(do) not　know　No　in　truth　I

ne　le　sais　pas...
not　it　know　-not-

J'avais　pourtant　assez　d'imagination　pour
I had　however　enough　-of- imagination　for

transformer cette morne cuisine en palais de
to transform this dull kitchen in palace of

marbre, en forêt enchantée, en jardin magique. Il
marble in forest enchanted in garden magic It

m'eût fallu peu d'efforts pour que les
had me been necessary (a) little -of- effort for that the

casseroles de cuivre s'animassent en fleurs
pans of copper themselves animated in flowers

magnifiques ; pour que le poulet mort ressuscitât
splendid ; for that the chicken dead rose again

en paon orgueilleux de son étincelante parure ;
in peacock proud with its sparkling finery ;

pour que le vase plein d'eau figurât une
for that the vase full of water should figure as a

source, un lac, une mer. Et Mariette elle-même,
spring a lake a sea And Mariette she herself

quelle difficulté à ce que,
what difficulty to this that

sous	le	coup	de	baguette	de	l'amour,	elle
under	the	blow	of	(the) stick	of	-the- love	she

m'apparût	comme	une	éblouissante	divinité,
appeared to me	like	a	dazzling	divinity

diadémée	d'étoiles,	et	trônant	sur	des	nuages ?
diadem	of stars	and	enthroned	on	-of- the	clouds ?

Ces	phénomènes	d'hallucination	daltonique	ne
These	phenomena	of hallucination	daltonique	not

sont	point	rares	chez	les	amoureux	et	les	poètes,
are	at all	rare	with	the	lovers	and	the	poets

pour	qui,	si	dénués	qu'ils	soient,	les	plus	pauvres
for	who	if	bared	that they	are	the	most	poor

serges	et	les	plus	calamiteux
serges worsted woollen cloths	and	the	more	calamitous

droguets	n'ont	point	de	peine	à	devenir,
droguets ribbed woollen dresses	not have	at all	-of-	trouble	to	become

subitement,	fastueux	brocarts,	tissus	d'or,	et
suddenly	sumptuous	brocades	tissues	of gold	and

pourpres royales. Les inconnues dont ils
purple   royal   The unknown persons which they

immortalisent, dans leurs poèmes, sur des
immortalize   in   their poems   on -of- the

fonds de paysage symbolique ou de colonnades
backgrounds of landscape symbolic or of colonnades

sardanapalesques, les vertus héroïques ou les
sardana-palesques the virtues heroic   or the

sanglantes luxures, n'ont été, le plus souvent,
bloody   lust   not have been the most often

que des êtres chétifs et répugnants,
(other) than -of the- beings puny and loathsome

Béatrix d'hôpital et Elvires de trottoir ; ou bien
Beatrix of hospital and Elvires of sidewalk ; or well

de patientes cuisinières, de roublardes
-of- patient cooks   -of- artful

maritornes, qui ont conquis l'âme du chantre
coarse ugly girls who have conquered the soul of the cantor

éthéré, par la sauce.
ethereal by the sauce

Il ne m'arriva rien de tel et je ne cherchai,
It not me arrived nothing of such and I not sought

dans cet amour, rien que le plaisir
in this love nothing (other) than the pleasure

physique, violent et nouveau qu'il me procurait.
physical violent and new that it me gave

À défaut de ce mensonge fastueux où ma
At fault of this lie sumptuous where my

vanité aurait pu se complaire à dresser,
vanity would have been able itself to please to rise

idole de mystère, de débauche ou de sacrifice,
idol of mystery of debauchery or of sacrifice

l'image surhumanisée de Mariette, j'aurais
the image made more than human of Mariette I would have

pu, du moins, me servir de cette créature de
been able of the least me serve of this creature of
at

133

Dieu pour y répandre mes effusions, mes
God for there spread my effusions my

inquiétudes et toutes les ardeurs intellectuelles
worries and all the ardors intellectual

que le silence, depuis si longtemps, depuis
that the silence since so (a) long time since
such

l'éveil de ma conscience, avait accumulées en
the awakening of my consciousness had accumulated in

moi. J'aurais pu me payer cette illusion
me I would have been able myself to pay this illusion

ennoblissante de faire de cette petite souillon la
ennobling by to make of this little slut the

confidente et la conseillère de mon âme. Jamais
confidante and the advisor of my soul Never

je n'avais parlé à personne, jamais personne
I not had spoken to anyone never anyone

n'avait été quelque chose pour moi. Mon père, ma
not had been some thing for me My father my

mère, mes sœurs, c'étaient moins que des
mother my sisters They were less than -of the-

passants, moins que les arbres et moins que les
passersby less than the trees and less than the

cailloux, lesquels ne protestent pas quand on
pebbles which not protest -not- when one

se confie à eux, et qui recueillent, sans
himself entrusts to them and who gather without

rire, les larmes de ceux qui pleurent.
to laugh the tears of those who mourn

L'occasion était bonne — il me le semble
The opportunity was good — It me it seems

maintenant — de transvider le trop-plein de mon
now — of to overflow the too-full of my

cœur dans un cœur qui m'appartenait. Eh bien !
heart in a heart which belonged to me Eh well !

je n'y songeai pas une minute. Non que je
I not there thought -not- (for) a minute Not that I
not of it

trouvasse excessif et ridicule d'attribuer ce rôle
found (it) excessive and ridiculous -of- to attribute this role

à une fille stupide, qui en eût été fort
to a girl stupid who of it had been very

embarrassée. Mais, c'est qu'en vérité mes
embarrassed But it is that in truth my

inquiétudes avaient disparu, et je ne sentais
worries had disappeared and I not felt

plus la nécessité d'effusions autres que celles
(any)more the need of effusions other than those

de mon sexe, de pénétrations autres que celles de
of my gender of penetrations other than those of

sa chair. Tout ce par quoi j'avais été, jadis, si
her flesh All this by what I had been back then so

ému, si tourmenté : mes adorations mystiques,
moved so tormented : my adorations mystical

mes tendresses panthéistes, mes enthousiasmes
my tendernesses pantheistic my enthusiasms

confus, mes élans désordonnés vers des poésies
confused my spirits disorderly towards of the poetries
airs

imprécises et violentes, et les énigmes
unclear and violent and the puzzles

angoissantes de toute la vie, et la terreur du
distressing of all the life and the terror of the

ciel nocturne, tout cela qui avait été mon
sky nocturnal all that which had been my

enfance, tout cela, aujourd'hui, se résumait
childhood all that today itself summed up

nettement, impitoyablement, dans l'unique désir
clearly pitiless in the only desire

charnel.
carnal

Je crois bien que jamais je n'adressai une seule
I believe well that never I not addressed a single

parole tendre à Mariette. Et nous n'éprouvions
word tender to Mariette And we not experienced

pas   le   besoin, moi de la dire, elle de l'entendre.
-not-   the   need   me of it to say she of it to hear

Ce petit argot des sentimentalités bébêtes et
This little slang of the sentimentality silly and
           speak

naïves par quoi j'avais débuté de la séduire —
naive through what I had started of her to seduce —
      with which

de la séduire ! — je ne l'employai plus dans
of her to seduce ! — I not it employed (any)more in

nos rencontres, presque quotidiennes, ni aucun
our encounters almost daily nor any

autre argot, ni aucun autre langage. Elle non plus,
other slang nor any other language She not either

si bavarde avec les autres, elle que le saut d'une
so talkative with the others she that the jump of a

mouche faisait rire aux larmes, ne me disait
fly made laugh to the tears not me said

jamais rien, sinon, avec terreur, lorsqu'on
ever nothing if not with terror when one

entendait du bruit dans la maison, ceci : «
heard / of the / noise / in / the / house / this / :

Prenez garde, monsieur Georges...
Take / guard / Mr. / Georges

c'est Monsieur ». Ce n'était pas toujours
this is / Mr. / This / not was / -not- / always
it is the master (of the house) / ever

Monsieur, ce n'était rien qu'un
Mr. / this / not was / nothing / than a
the master (of the house)

craquement de meuble, ou le grattement d'un rat
creaking / of / furniture / or / the / scratching / of a / rat

mangeant, dans l'office, à côté de nous, un
eating / in / the office / at / (the) side / of / us / a

reste de fromage. Quand je venais dans la cuisine,
rest / of / cheese / When / I / came / in / the / kitchen

elle savait pourquoi, et se préparait, sans joie,
she / knew / why / and / herself / prepared / without / joy

sans emportement, avec méthode et
without / passion / with / method / and

ponctualité. On eût dit que cela faisait partie de
punctuality One had said that that made part of

son service, comme de mettre les bifteaks sur le
her service like of to put the steaks on the

gril ou de balayer la salle à manger. D'ailleurs, je
grill or of to sweep the room to eat Anyway I
dining room

n'aimais à me trouver près d'elle qu'aux
did not like to me find near of her (other) than at the

heures du Désir. Et le Désir satisfait, je m'en
hours of the Desire And the Desire satisfied I me of it

allais, silencieux, ainsi que j'étais venu. Elle se
went silent as that I was come She herself
I had

remettait à son ouvrage, en imprimant à ses
handed over to her work in printing to her
would hand over

jupes un petit mouvement, comme font les poules
skirts a little movement like make the hens

qui se secouent après l'attaque brutale du
which themselves shake after the attack brutal of the

coq.
rooster

Cependant, j'étais jaloux d'elle, et lorsque je la
However I was jealous of her and when I her

voyais parler et rire avec les fournisseurs, surtout
saw speak and laugh with the providers especially

avec le menuisier dont elle savourait les grosses
with the carpenter of which she relished the rude

plaisanteries et l'obscène gaieté, cela me causait
jokes and the obscene gaiety that me caused

un véritable déplaisir et presque une souffrance.
a true displeasure and almost a pain

Cela dura six mois ainsi, sans heurts, sans
That lasted six months thus without clashes without

alertes, sinon que mon père me regardait avec
alerts if not that my father me watched with

plus d'obstination que de coutume.
more -of- obstinacy than -of- usual

Un soir, ma mère s'était rendue à l'église
One evening my mother herself was returned to the church
had

où se célébrait l'office du mois de Marie. Il
where itself celebrated the office of the months of Marie It

ne faisait pas nuit encore, et le crépuscule était
not made -not- night still and the dusk was
was

charmant et très doux. Il rôdait dans la
charming and very sweet It prowled in the
There

maison une odeur puissante de lilas. Mon père
house a smell strong of lilacs My father

devait être au jardin en train de chasser les
must be at the garden in train of to chase (away) the

escargots. Je me rendis à la cuisine. Mariette
snails I myself went to the kitchen Mariette

n'y était pas. Je la cherchai dans les autres
not there was -not- I her sought in the other

pièces, je la cherchai dans toute la maison.
rooms I her sought in whole the house

Vainement. Alors, je descendis au jardin. Mon
In vain — Then — I — descended — to the — garden — My

père non plus n'y était pas. Je fis le tour
father — not — either — not there — was — -not- — I — made — the — turn

des allées et des massifs, vainement. Je pensai
of the — walkways — and — of the — massifs / large blocks — in vain — I — thought

que mon père était peut-être sorti. Mais elle,
that — my — father — was — maybe — gone out — But — she

Mariette, où donc était-elle ? Un peu surpris et,
Mariette — where — then — was she — ? — A — bit — surprised — and

le dirai-je, mordu par la jalousie, je retournai à
it — I will say — bitten — by — the — jealousy — I — returned — to

la cuisine, et là, je remarquai que Mariette
the — kitchen — and — there — I — noticed — that — Mariette

avait laissé son souper inachevé.
had — left — her — supper — unfinished

— Le menuisier sera venu, songeai-je... Elle sera
— The — carpenter — will be come / will have — I thought — She — will be

allée quelque part avec lui...
gone   some   side   with   him

Je me dirigeai vers la grille, en faisant un
I myself headed towards the gate in making a

détour par la basse-cour. Si je ne la trouvais
turn by the low-court If I not her found

pas dans la basse-cour, peut-être l'apercevrais-je
-not- in the low-court maybe I would spot her

sur la route, en train de gaminer avec
on the road in (the) process of to kid around with

des hommes, avec ce maudit menuisier dont
-of- the men with this damn carpenter of which

je me plaisais à exagérer les qualités de
I myself liked to exaggerate the qualities of

séduction. Et voilà que, devant la porte de la
seduction And see there that in front of the door of the

grange, je vis le chien, assis sur son derrière, et
barn I saw the dog seated on his behind and

qui flairait obstinément le seuil. Il ne se
who sniffed stubbornly the threshold He not himself

dérangea pas à mon approche. Je connaissais sa
disturbed -not- at my approach I knew his

manière de sentir les rats et les souris, et je
way of to smell the rats and the mice and I

compris tout de suite que ce qu'il flairait en
understood all of following that this that he sniffed in

ce moment, ce n'étaient point des bestioles
this moment these not were at all of the critters

ordinaires.
ordinary

— Mariette est là ! me dis-je... Elle est là,
— Mariette is there ! me said I She is there

avec le menuisier.
with the carpenter

Et, pour la première fois, je ressentis au cœur
And for the first time I experienced at the heart

comme un coup.
like   a   blow

Je fis   quelques pas, doucement, sans bruit ;
I   made some   steps softly   without noise ;

puis   écartant   le   chien avec   d'adroites
Then   putting aside the   dog   with   dexterous

précautions, je   m'approchai de   la   porte, et
precautions I   myself approached of the door   and

j'y   collai mon oreille.
I there glued   my   ear

D'abord, je   n'entendis   que   mon cœur qui
Of first I   not heard   (other) than my   heart which
Initially

battait. Ensuite, un   bruit se précisa, un bruit
beat   Subsequently a   noise itself clarified a   noise

de paille remuée. On   eût dit que des   bottes de
of straw   stirred   One had said that of the boots of

paille dégringolaient les unes sur les autres.
straw   tumbled   the ones on   the others

Ensuite, une voix, une voix étouffée, dont il
Subsequently a voice a voice choked of which it

me fut impossible de distinguer si c'était une voix
me was impossible of to distinguish if it was a voice

d'homme ou de femme... Ensuite, deux voix
of man or of woman Subsequently two voices

ensemble, deux voix étouffées, deux voix qui
together two voices smothered two voices who

semblaient rire, ou pleurer, ou râler, je ne savais.
appeared to laugh or cry or bitch I not knew

Et, tout à coup, n'y tenant plus, impatient
And all to strike not there holding (any)more impatient
    all of a sudden not it

de surprendre ces deux voix, dont l'une me
of to surprise these two voices of which the one me

semblait être celle de Mariette, je poussai la
seemed to be that of Mariette I pushed the

porte d'un coup de poing furieux, et j'entrai dans
door with a blow of fist furious and I entered in

la grange. Mais l'étonnement — plus que de
the barn But the astonishment — more than -of-

l'étonnement — une sorte de terreur m'arrêta sur
the astonishment — a kind of terror stopped me on

le seuil ; et je vis, dans la pénombre que
the threshold ; and I saw in the twilight that

dorait un reste de jour pénétrant, avec moi, par
gilded a rest of day penetrating with me through

la porte ouverte, je vis mon père se dresser,
the door opened I saw my father himself raise up

hirsute, blême, et retenant, de ses deux mains,
shaggy pale and holding with his two hands

ses habits en désordre, tandis que Mariette,
his clothes in disorder while that Mariette

effarée, et la poitrine nue, s'efforçait de
frightened and the breast nude herself made efforts -of-
tried

plonger, pour   y   disparaître, dans un gouffre de
to plunge   for there to disappear   in   a   chasm   of

paille.
straw

Je restai   là   quelques secondes, ne sachant pas
I remained there   some   seconds   not knowing -not-

si je devais   avancer   ou bien m'enfuir ; à la fin,
if I   must   move forward or   well myself flee ; at the end

je pris ce dernier parti.
I took this   last   action

Le lendemain, mon père   m'aborda,   au jardin.
The following day   my   father approached me   at the garden
                                              in the

Il me donna vingt francs, et, sans me regarder,
He me   gave twenty franks   and without me to look at

il me dit :
he me said :

— Hier... dans la grange... oui, tu sais bien,
— Yesterday   in   the   barn   yes you know well

hier...   il   y   avait une fouine... Je la cherchais...
yesterday it there had   a   marten   I her was looking for

tu comprends... Voilà, je la cherchais... Et puis,
you   understand   See there I her was looking for And   then

il ne   faut   pas... en   parler à   ta   mère...
it not is necessary -not- of it to speak to your mother

parce que ta mère... tu comprends... a   peur
because that your mother you   understand   has fear

des fouines... Ça la tracasserait...
of the   martens That her   would bother

Et je vis, sur son front, de   grosses gouttes de
And I saw on his face -of-   large   drops   of

sueur rouler...
sweat   roll

www.ingramcontent.com/pod-product-compliance
Lightning Source LLC
LaVergne TN
LVHW011331080426
835513LV00006B/292